Rei

I WILL PREVAIL

Prophetic Declaration and Prayers to Command the Year, 2022

DANIEL C. OKPARA

Fasting And Breakthrough Prayers For the Year

A 21 Days Fasting and Prayers to Speak to the Year, Receive Direction and Provoke Restoration, Favor, and Breakthrough

TO EDIFY, HEAL, AND BLESS

The author provides the content of this book in good faith: to enlighten, encourage, and heal. He believes that when the subject discussed is followed, it will produce healing, divine intervention, and miracles from God. However, he does not intend his revelations to take the place of professional counseling and suggestions in your life. Neither is the teaching in this book supposed to be a doctrine to alter your faith in Christ. The author is sure and believes you will be blessed reading this book. However, he will bear no responsibility for any adverse consequences from any wrong understanding and application of the subject taught in this material. He prays, though, that you will make good use of the teaching and increase your faith in God.

Rehoboth 2022

Published By:

Better Life Media.

BETTER LIFE WORLD OUTREACH CENTER.

Website: www.BetterLifeWorld.org

Email: info@betterlifeworld.org

FOLLOW US ON FACEBOOK

Like our Page on Facebook for updates:

www.facebook.com/drdanielokpara

This title and others are available for quantity discounts for sale promotions, gifts, and evangelism. Visit our website or email us to get started.

All texts, calls, letters, testimonies, and inquiries are welcome.

BE EMPOWERED ON SOCIAL MEDIA

Day 235 of 365

Today, God says...

"He has begun a good work in your life, and He will bring it to perfection. He will not abandon you half way. Yes, you have had problems, drawbacks, challenges, and red sea situations, but He will see you through. Your setback is temporary. It is a setup for God's work in your life. Only believe. Everything about you will end in praise."

DR. DANIEL OKPARA | WORD4TODAY | DAY 235

Who says you can't use social media and still keep your spirit healthy for God? Follow me on Facebook for powerful daily broadcasts and prayers to stir your soul for Jesus every day and command your breakthrough.

www.facebook.com/drdanielokpara

RECEIVE WEEKLY PRAYERS

Powerful Prayers Sent to Your Inbox Every Monday

Enter your email address to receive notifications of new posts, prayers and prophetic declarations sent to you by email.

Email Address

Sign Me Up

Go to breakthroughprayers to subscribe to receive free weekly prayer points and prophetic declarations sent to you by email.

www.breakthroughprayers.org

FREE BOOKS

Take your relationship with God to a new level. Download these four powerful books for free and start a spiritual revolution in your life.

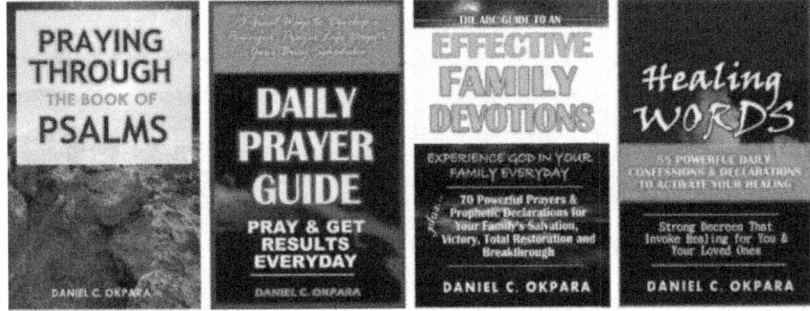

The link to download the books are at the end of this book

CONTENTS

OPENING PRAYER

Heavenly Father, I thank You for the blessing of another year. Thank You for Your protection and provision. And thank You for the opportunity that a new year brings for us.

It is only by Your mercy and grace that I have the opportunity to see this year, and for this, I say thank You, Lord.

This year, O Lord, help me through Your Spirit to grow in the knowledge of Your Word. Help me to walk in Your will and purpose for my life. And help me to seek Thy presence every day.

May my heart be drawn to heed the Your call. And cause me to walk in obedience every day, this year, in Jesus name.

Amen.

HOW TO USE THIS BOOK

This book is a guide to help you devote twenty-one days in reflection and prayers to surrender the new year to God. The prayers will help you encounter God like never before. They will guide you to present everything about you to Him.

You can use this book to pray any time of the year. Even though it is recommended to be used in the first and quarter of the year, I understand that not everyone will discover the book at the same time. While some people may read the book in January, February, or March, others may discover it in June, July, August, September, October, or November. Whenever you're able to pray with this book is perfectly okay.

If you found the book early enough and decided to pray with it in December, before the new year, that's great. If you found it in January, February, or March, that's also wonderful. And if it's in May, June, July, August, September, or October that you found it and decided to pray with it, you're in order. The point is that you understand the need to humble yourself and present everything about the year to God in prayers.

FASTING

As usual, follow this prayer guide with fasting for twenty-one days. Fasting helps us to tame the flesh and grow our spirits.

As I've always said, it's not the type of fasting that matters. I recommend doing whatever fasting your time, schedule, and present health condition can afford. Whether it's 6-10 or 6-6, choose the nature of fasting convenient for you.

Sometimes skipping dinner and staying awake to pray in the night is a good fast. Sometimes, too, ignoring social media and TV to read the Word, meditate, pray and listen to God only is the fast you need.

If you are led to do many days of fasting at a stretch, consider drinking water or juice along. Remember that our goal in fasting is to humble ourselves before God, not to prove a point or have something to brag about in the future.

PRAYER TIMES

While you may read and pray the prayers in this book at any time, my recommended best times to pray are as follows:

- 12:00am - 1:00am (Midnight Session)
- 3:00am - 4:00am (Early Morning Session)
- 6:00am – 7:00am (Morning Session)
- 12:00 – 1:00pm (Midday Session)
- 3:00pm – 4:00pm (Afternoon Session)
- 9:00pm – 10:00pm (Night Session)

You may choose any of the sessions and pray for twenty-one days. There are no musts, so whatever fits your schedule is welcome. If you prefer an afternoon session today and a night session tomorrow, you're in line. The most important thing is to expect the power of God to move in your life as you pray with me.

REMEMBER THIS

"Our goal in fasting is to humble ourselves before God, not to prove a point or have something to brag about in the future."

FOREWORD

Is This Another Year of Troubles?

Welcome to the year 2022. Let's start by saying thanks to God that we are here irrespective of the many challenges of years 2020 and 2021. I believe the Scripture, *"It is not of him that willeth, nor of him that runneth, but of the Lord that showeth mercy,"* now has a more substantial meaning to many of us today. We're slowly admitting that, yes, we may have control of things, but not in the way scientists and motivational speakers say it. We need God's mercy and help always.

I love science. And thank God for the good it has achieved and continues to achieve in our world. However, it is becoming more and more evident that, even with science, man is incapable of designing his path to fulfillment and happiness.

The Psalmist said:

> There is no real help or security in the hills and mountains. The help we need can only come from God (Psalm 121: 1 Paraphrased).

And this is where the problem is. As long as the world does not accept that we need God's help, the world will continue to stumble and fall. As long as the world does not think God should be part of the answers to its problems, we will continue to have issues that we cannot handle.

Look at this: someone is having a problem with his car; he goes to the maker of the car and says, *"Hey, I know you made this toy. I've got some problems trying to run it. But don't worry, I don't want you to help me. I will continue trying to figure my way out of the problem."*

That's the world's attitude to God. We're trying to figure our way out without recourse to what He, the creator of the world, says. And with that kind of approach, it's safe to say that no matter what we achieve as a solution to a problem, new problems that mystify us will always emerge. We cannot run the world without the help of the maker of the world. Sometimes, we even create bigger problems while trying to solve a problem.

This is not swearing; neither is it a pessimistic prophet-of-doom kind of view. It is the way it is. Every year, issues and situations that the world will struggle with will always emerge.

So, is this going to be another year of trouble?

Your answer is the same as mine.

Jesus said:

> "I have told you these things so that in Me you may have perfect peace and confidence. In the world, you will have tribulation and trials and distress and frustration...." (John 16:33a AMP).

Read that verse again and again and take it to heart. That, right there, is the reason it shouldn't surprise us when the peace steps the world takes in every place never works out.

Only a few months ago, to the surprise of the world, America's decades of effort to bring peace in Afghanistan crumbled. All those years of support, training, and ultimate sacrifice, in the end, everything flopped. Why?

> ***When God is not the source and reason for the peace, it won't last.***

Flawless, lasting peace can only happen when we accept God's guidance and leadership. Without that, any peace the world presents will not last.

"Dan, what are you saying?"

My message in this *foreword* is simple: Don't expect the problems in the world to diminish or be finally over. Don't expect things to eventually come back to normal. Don't expect a nation and a world where we will have peace, love for one another, and free prosperity for all.

This year, expect that there will be new issues to grapple with. As long as the world rejects the Prince of peace, she will always have problems she cannot handle.

BUT FEAR NOT

Yes, things will not get better in the world. Each year, the world's problems will outweigh and overwhelm her. However, as followers of Christ, we must not be afraid. God has promised to be with us. He has promised to be our light in the darkness.

> **The water that destroyed the world was the same water that saved Noah and his household.**

We have an assurance of peace and protection in Christ. He said, *"...Be of good cheer; take courage; be confident, certain, and undaunted! For I have overcome the world. I have deprived it of power to harm you and have conquered it for you"* (John 16:33b AMP).

Even if the world crumbles, God will keep us safe. He will surround those who trust in Him as the mountains surround Jerusalem. He will ensure that our going out and coming in is blessed.

As long as we continue to trust Him and not on our skills and wisdom, He will help us. Every day, His grace and mercy will speak for us, and His light will shine on us always.

REMEMBER THIS

> *"Flawless, lasting peace can only happen when we accept God's guidance and leadership. Without that, any peace the world presents will not last."*

INTRODUCTION

The Power and Blessings of Prayer-Planning Your New Year

Psalm 37: 5 - Commit everything you do to the LORD. Trust him, and he will help you (NLT).

Proverbs 16:3 - Commit to the LORD whatever you do, and he will establish your plans (NIV).

I discovered the truth of these scriptures in my life years ago. As a reader of motivational books, I would sit down every December and write out beautiful plans for the upcoming year. After writing my goals out, I would be full of faith in what I would do and achieve. However, by the following December, it would be evident that I realized less than 20% of everything I wrote down.

This kept happening until I began to ask myself questions:

- Writing out yearly plans and goals, is it really necessary?

- If we don't have control over our lives and what will happen tomorrow, why should I be listing things I want to do tomorrow?

- Shouldn't I just take life as it comes instead of listing the many things I would do and never do more than two out of ten?

- What's the best way to plan my life yearly?

- What goals should I even chase yearly?

As I kept reasoning within myself, the Holy Spirit began to show me that planning wasn't the problem. The problem was planning without thought to God's direction and guidance. He reminded me of the scripture that says, *"Unless the Lord builds the house, the laborers labor in vain."*

> **Unless we plan our lives with God, we are not guaranteed success.**

God is not saying, *"Don't plan your life."* Neither is He saying, *"Do nothing; sit down and wait for me to send you a written paper of things to do every year."* He is not saying, *"Just have faith; don't strategize."*

Not at all.

The Bible says, "We can make our plans, but the Lord determines our steps (Prov. 16:9 NLT)

This means you should plan your life, but do it in recognition of God's place in your life. Plan with Him. Do it prayerfully and surrender everything to Him. That is the difference between the believer and the nonbeliever.

There are two things this level of understanding will do in your life. First, it will keep you attentive in your spirit. You won't be excessively strict with your written plans since you know that God may want other things there. As you live your life through the year, you'll be in tune with God's Spirit. If He drops any new idea, goal, or vision in your spirit, you'll pick it and run with it, despite what you wrote down in your New Year goals.

Second, you'll be joyful no matter how much you didn't achieve. This is not saying that you won't make genuine efforts. You will. But you already know that God is committed to helping you accomplish only what matters. So, you will not let anything steal your joy because some things didn't come to pass as you planned them.

In 2021, for instance, God helped us acquire a landed property around May/June, and with His help, we built a mini tent for worship in October. But guess what, that wasn't a part of my plans for the year.

Yes, we wanted to leave the place we used for fellowship because it became increasingly uncomfortable for us. But we were looking for another rented space. That was all we saw and wanted. And that was what I went for.

We searched almost everywhere around our city and didn't find a space. Even when we wanted to use a hotel hall, they would agree on an amount today and change it as soon as we wanted to pay.

In the process, we casually began to look for land. It didn't make sense, but that ended up happening. With God's help, we got the land, and that's where we fellowship for now.

You see, God has the right to add to or subtract from your plans. That's how to achieve what matters, and that's why we must plan with Him.

YOU WILL NOT FAIL

Statistics say that 80% of people who draw new year goals and resolutions fail to achieve them. By

February, the majority had lost the grit for their New Year goals and resolutions and reverted to their status quo.

But what if you planned with God and somehow knew that the things on your list have some eternal significance? First, you'll find enough reasons to push through. And second, you'll find divine help along the way.

This awareness is why we come before God to prayer-plan the year in His presence. During this period of praying, fasting, meditation, and seeking, we present the year to Him, ask Him for what we should focus on, speak into the year, and surrender our desires to Him. We remind Him of His promises, "commit to Him whatever we want to do," and look up to Him to help us do much more than we asked or thought.

While you may not have a 100% success rate with your yearly plans this way, you will have more fulfillment, more joy, more happiness, more free time, and make more impact in the lives of others. You'll then realize that fighting to succeed is not the goal of life. Living in His plans is the biggest deal of life.

> ***Praying and seeking God's direction and following His plans will make your life more exciting, more fun, sometimes more challenging, but more fulfilling.***

Join me in this book to speak into the New year. Join me, and let's surrender our goals and New Year's resolutions to Him. Let's pray and say, *"Lord, guide our hearts on what we must pursue this year."* That's how to have a fulfilling year.

REMEMBER THIS

"Fighting to succeed is not the goal of life. Living in God's plans is the biggest deal of life."

SCRIPTURE FOR THE YEAR

Genesis 26: 12-22 (NKJV)

MEDITATE AS YOU READ

₁₂ Then Isaac sowed in that land, and reaped in the same year a hundredfold; and the Lord blessed him. ₁₃ The man began to prosper, and continued prospering until he became very prosperous; ₁₄ for he had possessions of flocks and possessions of herds and a great number of servants. So the Philistines envied him.

₁₅ Now, the Philistines had stopped up all the wells which his father's servants had dug in the days of Abraham, his father, and they had filled them with earth. ₁₆ And Abimelech said to Isaac, "Go away from us, for you are much mightier than we."

17 Then Isaac departed from there and pitched his tent in the Valley of Gerar and dwelt there. 18 And Isaac dug again the wells of water which they had dug in the days of Abraham his father, for the Philistines had stopped them up after the death of Abraham. He called them by the names which his father had called them.

19 Also, Isaac's servants dug in the valley and found a well of running water there. 20 But the herdsmen of Gerar quarreled with Isaac's herdsmen, saying, "The water is ours." So he called the name of the well Esek because they quarreled with him.

21 Then they dug another well, and they quarreled over that one also. So he called its name Sitnah.

22 And he moved from there and dug another well, and they did not quarrel over it. So he called its name **Rehoboth** because he said, "For now the Lord has made room for us, and we shall be fruitful in the land."

REMEMBER THIS

> *₂₂And he moved from there and dug another well, and they did not quarrel over it. So he called its name <u>Rehoboth</u> because he said, "For now the Lord has made room for us, and we shall be fruitful in the land."*

SECTION ONE

NEW YEAR PROPHETIC THEME PRAYERS

This section contains teachings, prophetic exhortations, and prayers based on our theme for the year. Expect a powerful release of God's presence in your life as we pray.

DAY 1

GRATITUDE CHECK

---

1 Chronicle 16:34 - Oh, give thanks to the Lord, for He is good! For His mercy endures forever

---

Once again, welcome to the year of the Lord, AD 2022. It is, for us, a year the Lord has made, and we will rejoice and be glad in it.

I know. There may be situations in your life that didn't come out as you planned last year and the previous years. There may be prayer requests that didn't get the attention you earnestly wanted. Nevertheless, if you are reading this, God is good to you.

So, before we start praying the prophetic words for this year, come before God with thanks.

GOD IS AT WORK IN YOUR LIFE

One of the most challenging lessons I've learned is that God is at work in our lives no matter what happened and what didn't happen. As I shared on my Facebook page:

> *"Even when we are hurting, facing setbacks, and delay; even when we don't feel good about God and are wondering when our change will happen, God is at work in our lives."*

Your prayers are working; your seeds of faith are working. Your waiting and believing are preparing you for what God has in store for your life. Everything is coming together. God is growing and developing you little by little. And surely, everything will work out for your good.

WHY GIVE THANKS?

It's New Year, and we are planning for the New Year in power. But what happened in the past year? From January to December, was God good to you? What are twelve remarkable things you are grateful to God for?

Don't continue reading until you list them out. If there are more, great. List them out. But they cannot be less than twelve. Each one represents a month of the year.

You need to mention at least twelve specific gratitude assessments as we proceed in this prayer. Then you need to spend time thanking God for each one of them. That's what I call a gratitude check.

12 GRATITUDE CHECKS

1. ....

2. ....

3. ....

4. ....

5. ....

6. ....

7. ....

8. ....

9. ....

10. ....

11. ....

12. ....

DON'T FOCUS ON WHAT IS NOT DONE

Psalm 77:11 - I will remember the deeds of the Lord; yes, I will remember your miracles of long ago. I will consider all your works and meditate on all your mighty deeds.

When we recall God's mighty acts in the past, we are proclaiming our faith in His future deliverance. If God were good to us yesterday, He would be good today and tomorrow.

> *Recalling past victories and remembering that God has been faithful in the past is the key to having a glorious future.*

Don't focus on what is not done to the extent that you forget what is done. As I teach in our Church, "Sometimes, look away from what is yet to be done, and focus on what He has done and what He is doing. That is how to receive answers to what needs to be done."

Someone said, "Even if you lost something, God is the reason you didn't lose everything." So, give thanks.

Stop letting unmet needs kill your joy of thanking God for what He has done and what He is doing.

Start this prayer retreat by doing a gratitude check. Spend time and thank God for at least twelve reasons.

THE SACRIFICE OF PRAISE

And if praising and thanking God seems difficult in your life because of the difficulties you're going through, then remember something called *"the sacrifice of praise."* It means to give thanks even when it seems there isn't much to be thankful for.

Paul and Silas were thrown in jail for preaching the gospel and casting out a demon. One would expect them to be worried about how God did not intervene to prevent such a thing from happening. But they praised God instead. That's a sacrifice of praise.

> By him, therefore, let us offer the sacrifice of praise to God continually, that is, the fruit of our lips giving thanks to his name – **Hebrews 13:15**

Today, declare God's praise. Declare His goodness, mercy, and love. Declare your appreciation for the gift of another year, a new beginning, a new opportunity, and a new hope.

Shout it: "The Lord is good! His mercy endures forever."

PRAYERS/DECLARATIONS

PRAISE

Heavenly Father,

The God of all blessings, the source of all life, and the giver of all grace.

I thank You for the gift of life, for the breath that nourishes our lives, for the food that sustains us, and for family and community without which we would not exist.

Thank You, Lord, for Your protection and provision in the past year. Thank You for the new year that has come. And thank You for bringing us safely into the year.

Father, I praise You today and will do so forever and ever, in Jesus name

---

Father, thank You for the mystery of creation, for the beauty that the eyes can see, for the joy that the ears can hear, and for the unknown that we cannot behold.

Thank You for the massiveness of the universe that draws us beyond our definition and fills us with wonders.

Thank You for the mystery of communities and societies

Thank You for establishing the family system that nurtures our becoming.

Thank You for the opportunity of friendships.

Thank You for our children who lighten our moments with delight; for the unborn, who offer us hope for the future.

Thank You for strangers and for people from other nativities who make us wonder about the extent of the world and grow in knowledge.

O Lord, I thank You for this day, and for this year; thank You for life and for one more year to experience Your love and to work for justice and peace.

Thank You, Lord, for neighbors who keep us company and teach us patience. Thank You for those who love me and those who teach and empower me to love.

Thank You for a year to experience Your presence and live Your promise.

For everything You have done, everything You will do, all the blessings and lessons of the past, and lessons ordained for the present and future, I give You thanks, through Jesus Christ, I pray.

Amen

THANKSGIVING

I praise You, O Lord, for all that You have done for my family and me; You saved us from the lion's mouth, delivered us from the wild ox, and freed us from the devourer's cage.

You continue to protect and keep us safe in this dangerous world. Thank You for Your love and kindness every day.

Father, Lord, You did not despise nor detest me when I was afflicted; neither did You hide Your face from me.

I called on You severally; You answered and listened to me when I cried. You also helped me all through the year. For this, I declare that my praise will continually be of Thee.

I will praise You, Lord, before the world and before the congregation of Your people. And I will pay my vows made in the time of trouble,

*before those who fear You. Thank You,
everlasting Father, in Jesus name.*

PSALM 138:1-3

*"O Lord, our God, maker of heaven and earth.
You are the Lord God Almighty.*

*Your praise and glory fills the earth. Your
praise fills my life, and Your praise fills my
family.*

I thank You, Lord, with all my heart.

Today, I sing praise to You before the gods.

*I face Your holy Temple, bow down, and praise
Your name because of Your constant love and
faithfulness, because You have shown that Your
name and Your commands are supreme.*

*You answered me when I called to You; with
Your strength, You strengthened me.*

May Your name be praised forever and ever, in Jesus name

O Lord, even though You are so high above, You care for the lowly, and the proud cannot hide from You.

When troubles surround me, you keep me safe. You oppose my bitter enemies and save me by Your power.

You will do everything you have promised; Lord, Your love is eternal. You will complete the work that You have begun.

Be glorified, forever and ever

In Jesus name.

Amen.

REMEMBER THIS…

"Your waiting and believing are preparing you for what God has in store for your life."

DAY 2

DECLARATION FOR THE YEAR

"There will be famine, but there will also be abundance. There will be hardship, but there will also be ease. There will be travails, but there will also be comfort. Do not focus on the tribulations or get carried away by the travails. In the travails, you will prevail."

So, what is God saying for the year? What is this year's prophetic focus, and what should you do with it? Should you use only this message, or can you combine it with another prophetic declaration for the year? How about what God is laying in your heart for the year? How should you handle it?

Before I proceed with sharing what God is saying in my heart about the year 2022, let me give you a rundown of how we fared with our prophetic themes in the last two years. I'm adding this rundown to properly prepare your mind to receive this prophetic word.

MORE THAN A PRAYER POINT

In 2020, by the Holy Spirit, I declared to our community (the church, our books readers, subscribers, and our social media audience) that it was a year to *arise and shine*. This word came while praying and thinking about the year before our crossover service. God took me to Isaiah chapter 60, and as I studied and meditated on verses 1 and 2, I saw the rise of darkness in the land. Then I shared with our Church that darkness would spread in the land but that God would cause His light to shine upon us and through us. By the Holy Spirit, I declared the theme for the year as, *"I Will Arise And Shine."*

I remember using the words, "the devil has enough madness for everyone this year. But God will be our light. We will shine, even if a demonic madness spreads through the land."

Many of our church members have not forgotten the words, "satan's madness and God's victory." It was so used in our Church that year. However, in all honesty, when God gave me those words, I did not envisage the level of darkness that happened in 2020. My mind went to the usuals - insecurity, economic crisis, and terrorism - but not the dangerous plague that shook the world.

Thank God, though, that we're here irrespective of all that happened. God kept us for His purpose and glory.

Then enter 2021. As we were preparing for the year, God showed me a vision from the book of Genesis 1: 26-28. I saw the rise of evil powers around the world. Then God spoke to me and said, "Teach my people to know who they are in

Me and have dominion. Teach them to stand against the birds of the air, the beasts of the land, and the fishes in the water. Teach them to build up their most holy faith and refuse to fall for intimidations that would arise in their lives, in their communities, and the nations."

For the first time, while reading that scripture, I saw a deeper dimension of what it means to have dominion over the birds of the air, the beasts of the land, and the fishes in the seas. I saw that, beyond physical animals, God was referring to evil powers and systems. Even before they existed, God planned that we would rule and have dominion over them.

Yes, even before the drama in Eden and the fall of man, even before the emergence of the covenant eras and Christ's death, God formed us to rule and reign. We are made to have dominion. No witch has what it takes to destroy God's plan for our lives.

I published the message in our <u>New Year Prayers</u> collection with the title, *Dominion 2021.* And today, as I look back on the year's events, I see that the year had it full of intimidations from many fronts. Never have we seen the level of pressure that political powers pursued over their citizens.

While I may not know everything that happened in your country and how things fared, I'm sure that governments' intimidation rose and is still rising almost everywhere. As I write this, Russia is piling up an unprecedented amount of armory against Ukraine, and experts think this is too much intimidation. The crisis could spill onto the whole of Europe.

I don't even want to talk about my own country. The level of intimidation we experienced from our government in 2021 is the worse since I became an adult. People are arrested for saying things like *"We need good roads"* on Facebook. The army can come after you for posting something like, *"stop the bloodshed"* or saying, *"The president is incompetent."*

The citizens are treated as enemies, while terrorists are treated as special ones. And the media is forbidden from reporting what is happening. They even banned Twitter. It's so bad that, most times, we have to rely on foreign media to hear what happened in our backyards.

In all these things, though, we thank God who gives us victory. Through Christ, we will continue to walk in victory, in Jesus name.

STRONG SPIRITUAL ALERTS

Why am I boring you with these updates?

Well, as I was reflecting over these prophetic themes for the year, I had some *wow* moments. I observed that, even though the declarations were planned to be prayer guides, yearly events manifested to agree with them. Consequently, I have become even more assured that the Holy

Spirit is using these prophetic calls and prayers to keep me and our community prepared for God's purpose. They are more than just prayer points. They are powerful alerts to point us in the right direction of preparation for the year.

So, while the prophetic messages are not designed to predict expected events, they are solid alerts and preparation for us. While you should not think of the messages as a prediction, receive it, though, as a powerful call to build your faith and keep you aligned in God's heartbeat for the time.

> *This prophetic declaration is a timely message to keep you prepared to receive all that God has in store for you this year.*

Receive it with a ready heart and desire the positive outcomes it delivers.

And as you receive it, remember that "we know in part and prophesy in part," meaning that the word, though powerful, is still a part of the picture for 2022, not the only picture. So, if there are other voices that you submit to, listen to what God is saying through them. And don't forget to include what God is saying in your heart, too, for the year.

PROPHETIC THEME FOR THE YEAR

Now that you know how to receive this prophetic declaration for the year, what is God saying about the year? What is our theme for the year?

The Lord says:

> "There will be famine, but there will also be abundance. There will be hardship, but there will also be ease. There will be travails, but there will also be comfort. Do not focus on the tribulations or get carried away by the travails. In the travails, you will prevail.

"Focus on the comfort that rests in trusting God, for I will comfort those who look up to Me. My mercy will be upon them, and My grace will be sufficient for them. Their faces will be lightened, and their burdens will be made easy. When men say there is a casting down, you will say there is a lifting up."

And we say, "Praise the Lord! May the Word of God for our lives come to pass in abundance, in Jesus name."

Amen.

Now, let's talk about the message in-depth. Let's look at the various aspects of the prophetic word and break them down.

God is saying that there will be famine in 2022.

"What kind of famine?" you say.

Famine means scarcity, hardship, starvation, increase in needs and decrease in resources. It means being deprived of essential capabilities.

Famine means an increase in attacks on incomes and sources of provision. It means mass job loss and more suffering in the land.

Although the mystery of famine is already operating in the world, it will get even more severe as we approach the end of time. This year, expect an increase in the mystery of famine.

However, by our covenant alignment, we will prevail. That's the core of this message. There was also abundance in the same year that there was a famine in the land where Isacc dwelt.

So, God is saying: "Don't focus on the troubles and lose sight of the blessings. Sow your seeds in faith, not in fear. God will make a way. He has empowered you to prevail."

Therefore, by the inspiration of the Holy Spirit, I declare the year 2022 as the year *we will prevail*. It is our year of *Rehoboth*, which in our application means

- Empowered to prevail,
- Divinely qualified for growth, increase, and expansion,
- Excelling in the Famine
- I have room for expansion
- Diving opportunities for growth

Our anchor text says:

> "And he moved from there and dug another well, and they did not quarrel over it. So he called its name Rehoboth because he said, "For now the Lord has made room for us, and we shall be fruitful in the land" (Gen. 26:22).

This year, God has called you, against all odds, to prevail. Even if you encounter resistance over God's direction for your life, even if you see initial struggles over your resources, even if things initially happen to get you discouraged and fearful, God says you will prevail.

Don't focus on the problems. You are divinely empowered, and there are opportunities for growth and increase for you this year. You will not be a victim of the troubles in the land.

This year, keep your focus forward. Keep your focus on restoration, growth, increase, and victory - against all odds. You will prevail because God is with you and for you.

Declare with me:

"This year, 2022, I will prevail against all odds.

"It is my year of Rehoboth. No matter what happens in the land, I have the blessing and the power of God working in me and for me. Therefore, I will prevail.

"I will not pack up or go back to Egypt because of any famine in the land. I will keep trusting God, and where others are saying there's a casting down, I will be saying there's a lifting up.

"I will see growth and expansion like never before. And because God is with me, no one can stand against me, in the name of Jesus Christ.

PREVAILING IN THE TRAVAILS

This year, the enemy may try, but God will cause you to triumph. Like Isaac, under the covenant, you are empowered to shine in the famine. Though it was very hard for the nation where Isaac lived, he prevailed. So, even if things get very tough where you are, even if the famine is more severe than what we witnessed before, you will prevail.

In addition to the confusion trailing the COVID-19, new issues will arise to worry about. As Jesus already said, *"The hearts of men will fail."* But in all, those whose eyes are on Jehovah will prevail.

Trust God and remain focused. You will not be pushed up and down anyhow. When men are forced to say there is a casting down, the mystery at work in your life will empower you to be saying there is a lifting up.

PRAYERS/DECLARATIONS

This year (...), I will prevail.

Because I am in God's covenant.

I am a child of God through Christ.

I have the nature and image of God.

The Holy Spirit is in me.

The mystery that spoke in favor of Isaac during a national famine will speak for me this year, no matter what happens, in the name of Jesus Christ.

Before now, God has empowered me to excel and overcome.

Therefore, this year will be a year of victory and opportunity for me.

I will grow and expand in wisdom.

I will grow and expand in faith

I will grow and expand in love.

I will grow and expand in ministry.

I will grow and expand in possessions.

I will grow and expand in my finances.

I will grow and expand in miracles and thanksgiving.

It is my year of Rehoboth, in Jesus name.

The blessings of God are upon my life and home this year (...)

The earth will yield her increase for us.

Wherever we go and whatever we do, we will excel, and our influence will be visible to all.

Everything God has made is good, so this year will be good for me and my family.

We will not be victims of sickness, lack, scarcity, pain, terrorism, attacks, and death, in the name of Jesus Christ.

This year, (...), my peace, good health, and prosperity shall be enlarged.

Even if the evil powers of the heavenly, of the seas, and of the grounds are shaken, and famine covers the earth, and gross darkness the people, I, and my family will be spared.

Yes, I will be safe and secure.

My family will be safe and secure.

And we will excel and shine because the Spirit of God indwells us, and God's glory is being revealed upon us and through us.

This year (...), I will never be out of a job.

Jobs, opportunities, and openings will abound for me and my household.

And we will not labor in darkness.

Nations will come to our light.

Kings will come to see the glory of God upon me, and my testimony shall draw men and women unto the Lord.

This year, (...), my spouse and I shall grow stronger together.

Our children shall be drawn to the Lord, and all they connected to me shall be supernaturally protected, preserved, and provided for, in Jesus name.

This year (.....), the abundance of the sea shall be converted unto me.

The prosperity in the heavenly shall flow into my household.

And the blessings in the land will supernaturally locate me every day.

My vision, business, career, and contributions shall be recognized in high places.

And I shall be divinely recommended for promotion, celebration, and all kinds of good things, in Jesus name.

This year (...), I, my spouse, children, and everyone connected to me shall have an abundance of health, peace, love, and financial prosperity.

We will share with others the abundance of our supernatural supplies of wealth, peace, good health, and the message of salvation.

This year, we are distributors of kindness, goodness, peace, love, and all the fruit of the Holy Spirit.

This year (...), money shall serve my family and me.

Scarcity shall be far from us.

When others say there is not enough, we shall be sharing from God's excess in our care.

Through the mercies of God, we will find help and support in our times of need.

This year (…), all the broken places of my life will be rebuilt.

By God's strange intervention, I will experience restoration in every area of my life.

I will no longer lose anything in my life and family.

I will see restoration in my marriage, relationships, and career.

My children will call me blessed, and I shall be a blessing to them and everyone around us.

This year (……), I shall not fail in my assignment as a Christian.

I shall not fail in my job and relationship with others.

I shall have the wisdom to nurture what needs to be nurtured and uproot what needs to be uprooted, in Jesus name.

This year (....) I shall walk in divine favor every day.

I shall be re-accepted and doubly honored wherever I was rejected in the past.

Every respect, honor, and promotion that has eluded me in the past shall be restored to me.

I shall be a joy to behold.

People will feel blessed knowing and working with me.

And through me, lives will be made better, in Jesus name

All through this year (...), whatever I lay my hands to do shall prosper.

For brass, God will bring gold, and for iron, God will bring silver, and for wood brass, and for stones iron.

I shall walk in integrity, and righteousness and peace shall rule over mine habitation.

I will carry the presence of God in my office and company.

I will excel in the work of my hands, in the name of Jesus.

This year (......), there shall be no violence in my life and family.

Every plan to perpetrate crime, vandalism, terrorism, violence, and kidnapping around me is canceled.

There'll be no more stories of crime in and around me, no robberies, and no destruction, in Jesus name.

This year (…), my street shall be called salvation street, and peace shall reign in my neighborhood, in Jesus name

This year (…), I will arise and shine.

I will not sit in darkness nor remain in the valley.

I shall have victory in every area of my life.

I shall have victory in my family, workplace, ministry, and everywhere I go.

I shall have victory in my relationship, in Jesus name.

This year (…), nothing shall stop the work of the Holy Spirit in my life.

No weapon fashioned against me shall prosper, and every tongue that rises against me this year shall be condemned, in Jesus name.

This year, I decree that I am filled with power according to the order of Moses, Jesus, and the apostles.

I am a candidate for signs, wonders, and miracles. I will lay my hands on the sick, and they shall recover. I shall cast out devils, and even if I drink any deadly thing by mistake, it shall not hurt me, in Jesus name.

I am free from every form of ancestral curses, patterns, and problems from my bloodline.

I declare that there is no more room for any ancestral affliction in my life and family.

And may all open doors through which curses come and operate in my lineage be closed by the Blood of Jesus Christ, in Jesus name.

I confess and believe that this year is my year of Rehoboth.

It is my year of celebration and not a year of mourning.

I am walking from connection to connection, from blessing to blessing, from protection to protection, from power to power, and from victory to victory, in the name of Jesus Christ.

Amen.

REMEMBER THIS…

Even if things get very hard where you are, even if the famine is more severe than what we witnessed before, you will prevail.

DAY 3

BECAUSE THE LORD BLESSED HIM

Then Isaac sowed in that land, and reaped in the same year a hundredfold; and the Lord blessed him - Genesis 26: 12

The background of this story is that there was a famine in the land where Isacc lived. This was not the same famine that happened during his father's time. It was a new one.

A more modern description would be that "There was a new, serious, national crisis in Isaac's time. This is a different crisis from what happened in his father's time. This time, the meltdown was so severe that people could not find food."

Okay, let's use Scripture's exact words:

"There was a new famine, different from the previous one."

This should give you an idea of what's happening in the spirit here. It means that whatever we have seen before is small compared to what is coming. And it's not the same as the previous experience.

I'm not an alarmist, but Scripture is clear that the second famine was different from the first. This means that new issues other than what we already know will come up to confound man.

According to National Geographic, famines result in malnutrition, starvation, disease, and a high death rate. So, don't just look at the word *famine* as *no rain*. It is more than that.

There was starvation, outbreak, high death rate, loss of jobs, and nationwide uncertainty. That was the actual state of things in the nation where Isaac lived. That's the contents of the mystery of famine.

Famines can be caused by a natural disaster, such as flooding, cyclones, pest invasions, or an epidemic. A government's anti-people policies, failure, and poor decisions can also result in famines. Human events, such as war, political crisis, and riots can also cause famine.

Though the Bible did not precisely state the cause of the famine during the time of Isaac, it did say that the famine was severe. Thankfully, though, that same year, Isaac planted in the land.

Amid the crisis, he found the courage to sow seeds. It didn't make sense, but he stood on God's word and looked beyond what was happening. As a result, he reaped a hundred times as much as he planted in the same year because the Lord blessed and favored him.

God will bless and favor you this year. You will receive hundredfold returns in every area of your life, in Jesus name.

This story is a lesson that, sometimes, well-known systems can fail, and the government's efforts to help will be futile. Sometimes, nature can revolt against man's stubbornness.

> ***Don't consider it strange when governments cannot create jobs, reduce unemployment, provide security, and ensure economic progress.***

As I study the Word of God, observe the world, and meditate, I can tell you that our today's world will always be subject to the mystery of famine. Governments and established systems will constantly fail to meet the needs of the people. There will always be complaints here and there. And from time to time, there will be fear, helplessness, and hopelessness in the land.

However, we can hold onto the Word of God for our lives. The Word will not fail, even when our systems fail.

> **There is a covenant of exemption speaking over your life. Even when it's not so obvious due to the problems you face, it's there, and you must never let go of its consciousness.**

We are in the spiritual genealogy of Abraham, and God's covenant with him is extended to us. When others are crying that there's a casting down, we must look to the Word of God for our lives and stand on it. His grace is there for us to be saying there is a lifting up.

Lastly, every good thing we expect to happen to us this year will be because of the mercies and goodness of God. And that's what I want you to learn today. It won't be because of our knowledge, experience, certificate, connections, and abilities.

You will not make it through this year because of your human capability; neither will your smartness be enough to help you overcome the famine (and issues of life) we will witness in the world. Your victory will be because God is with you; His mercies and goodness speak over your life and family.

The same year that everyone was crying wolf, Isaac went out and sowed. The same land that was unproductive for others, Isaac's crops yielded a hundred times what he planted, and he became very wealthy.

But wait! It was **because God blessed him**. Not because he was the best worker in the land.

As we continue this prayer for the year, declare your trust in God. Yes, we will work. We will go out and sow, invest, and trade. But our success will be because of God's help, not because of our smartness. So, acknowledge God and declare that everything you expect this year is because you trust and believe in His ability, not yours.

MEDITATE ON THESE SCRIPTURES

Proverbs 3: 5-7 — ₅Trust in the Lord with all your heart, and lean not on your understanding; ₆ In all your ways acknowledge Him, and He shall direct your paths.

₇Do not be wise in your own eyes; fear the Lord and depart from evil. ₈It will be health to your flesh and strength to your bones.

Psalm 37: 3-6 — ₃Trust in the Lord, and do good; dwell in the land, and feed on His faithfulness. ₄ Delight yourself also in the Lord, and He shall give you the desires of your heart.

₅Commit your way to the Lord, trust also in Him, and He shall bring it to pass. ₆He shall bring forth your righteousness as the light, and your justice as the noonday.

Isaiah 26: 3-4 — ₃You will keep him in perfect peace, whose mind is stayed on You, because he trusts in You. ₄Trust in the Lord forever, for in Yah, the Lord, is everlasting strength.

Jeremiah 17: 5-8 - ₅Thus says the Lord: "Cursed is the man who trusts in man and makes flesh his strength, whose heart departs from the Lord. ₆For he shall be like a tree in the desert and shall not see when good comes, but shall inhabit the dry places in the wilderness, in a salt land which is not inhabited.

₇"Blessed is the man who trusts in the Lord and whose hope is the Lord. ₈For he shall be like a tree planted by the waters, which spreads out its roots by the river, and will not fear when heat comes; but its leaf will be green, and will not be anxious in the year of drought, nor will cease from yielding fruit.

Jeremiah 9:23 - This is what the LORD says: "Let not the wise man boast in his wisdom, nor the strong man in his strength, nor the wealthy man in his riches.

Proverbs 23: 4-5 (GNT) - 4 Be wise enough not to wear yourself out trying to get rich. 5 Your money can be gone in a flash, as if it had grown wings and flown away like an eagle.

PRAYERS/DECLARATIONS

Heavenly Father,

This year, I declare, again, that I put my trust in You. I remind myself that it is not by power, nor by might, that I will pull through but by the Holy Spirit.

O Lord, I proclaim that my confidence is in You, not on my own understanding, connection, or strength. I will not depend on my own strategies but on Your wisdom.

Father, help me to seek Your will in all that I do this year; show me which path to take in every situation. Cause me never to be satisfied with my wisdom and ability. Help me to turn away from evil and to walk in the path of holiness.

As I do, Lord, may Your healing always rest on my body and Your strength on my bones, in Jesus name.

I declare today, according to Psalm 37: 3-5, that I will trust in the Lord, and with His help, I will do good. He will cause me to dwell safely in the land and be fruitful at all times.

I will take delight in Him, and He will give me the desires of my heart.

Henceforth, as I commit to Him everything I do, I will be supernaturally helped in every area of my life, in Jesus name.

All through this year, my mind will focus on the Lord, God Almighty. He will keep me in perfect peace, and I shall not be moved irrespective of the famine and failures of our worldly systems.

Today, I denounce my dependence on the arm of flesh. I denounce my hope and trust in human solutions. My hope is in the Lord, and in Him alone, I put my trust.

This year, I shall be like a tree planted by the waters, spreading its roots by the river. I will not fear when the heat comes. My strength shall always be green. Even in drought and famine, I will not cease from bearing fruits, in Jesus name.

This year, my boast is in the Lord; my strength is of Him, and my wealth will flow from Him.

I will not wear myself out trying to make money or get rich. I will seek the kingdom of God and serve God with my spirit, soul, and body. As I do so, everything that makes life comfortable and meaningful will follow me, in the name of Jesus Christ.

This same year, my labor shall be increasingly blessed, so much that it will be said and shared that the hand of God is on my life.

This same year, as it was with Isaac, so shall it be with me. My efforts and seeds shall bear a hundredfold increase because the blessings of God are upon me, in Jesus name.

Amen.

REMEMBER THIS

There is a covenant of exemption speaking over our lives. Even when it's not so obvious due to the problems we face, it's there, and we must never let go of its consciousness.

DAY 4

IT'S MORE THAN A PROMISE; IT'S AN OATH

₁And there was a famine in the land, other than the former famine that was in the days of Abraham. And Isaac went to Gerar, to Abimelech, king of the Philistines.

₂And the Lord appeared to him and said, Do not go down to Egypt; live in the land of which I will tell you.

₃**Dwell temporarily in this land, and I will be with you and will favor you with blessings; for to you and your descendants I will give all these lands, and I will perform the oath which I swore to Abraham, your father.**

₄And I will make your descendants multiply as the stars of the heavens, and will give to your posterity all these lands (kingdoms); and by your offspring shall all the nations of the earth be blessed, or by Him bless themselves, ₅For Abraham listened to and obeyed My voice and kept My charge, My commands, My statutes, and My laws (Genesis 26: 1-5 AMPC)

As a believer and teacher of the Biblical concepts of deliverance, I am constantly inundated with prayer requests for deliverance from generational curses. The subject of generational curses has become so popular that, today, almost everyone talks about it in the body of Christ. However, in addition to knowing about generational curses, we also need to know about generational blessings.

If curses can move from one generation to another, then blessings can also move from one generation to another. In fact, the forces behind blessings are even more powerful than the forces behind curses.

In the verses we read today (see especially the bolded), God tells Isaac, *"Relax. Stay briefly in this land, and I will be with you and will favor you with blessings; for to you and your descendants I will give all these lands, and I will perform the oath which I swore to Abraham, your father."*

In other words, the blessings that Isaac experienced in verses 12 and 13, where he reaped a hundredfold return on his labor and became more prosperous than the country, was not only because he was smart and worked very hard. In addition to his faith, smartness, and hard work, there was a powerful oath speaking over his life, speaking in his favor, and ensuring that things turned out okay for him. That oath was the covenant God had with his father, Abraham.

All Isaac needed to activate that great oath was to listen and obey. As long as he was willing to obey, he would eat the good of the land, whether there was famine or not. Because his destiny, finances, and life were not tied to the economy of the land. He was a special case, under a special covering. And that covering, the covenant, was superior to the economy

BRIEFLY ABOUT THE OATH

Genesis 22: 15-18 — 15 Then, the angel of the Lord called again to Abraham from heaven. 16 "This is what the LORD says: Because you have obeyed me and have not withheld even your son, your only son, I swear by my own name that…

17 I will certainly bless you. I will multiply your descendants beyond number, like the stars in the sky and the sand on the seashore. Your descendants will conquer the cities of their enemies. 18 And through your descendants, all the nations of the earth will be blessed—all because you have obeyed me." (NLT)

Look at that again.

There's no way Isaac would not be blessed. God was under oath to bless His father's seed, and he was the seed. This sworn blessing was the foundation of his victories and successes during the famine. It was the oath that made the difference. For God says in Psalm 89:34:

My covenant I will not break nor alter the word that has gone out of My lips.

In the culture that Abraham grew from, an oath was the end of all disputes. For instance, if two people quarreled over the ownership of a piece of land, and the matter became severe, the community elders would ask the people in question to swear an oath. Knowing how sacred and powerful an oath is, the unsure and bullying person will most certainly withdraw from the dispute. If not, he will be killed by the forces before whom the oath was administered.

To an extent, this type of justice system is still used in many cultures and communities across the world. It is still used in my culture. An oath brings to an end all disputes. It is not a light thing before God and man.

An oath is different and more potent than a simple promise. Oaths are sacred commitments, often invoking divine witnesses regarding one's future action or behavior. When you swear an oath, you invoke invisible powers to witness the truth of what you are saying or to witness that you sincerely intend to do what you are saying.

When God promised to bless Abraham, to end all questions, fears, and disputes about the feasibility and practicability of what He was telling him, He swore an oath. After all, how do you convince a 99-year old adult that he would bear a son and his children would possess the earth? God had to swear an oath to Abraham. And because there was no one greater for Him to swear by, He swore by himself (Heb. 6:13).

This means, come rain, come shine, God is committed to keeping His oath with Abraham.

The oath (covenant) was not just a promise. It was more than that.

And the good news today is that, through Christ, we are the spiritual descendants of Abraham.

> **Galatians 3: 26-29** — ₂₆For you are all children of God through faith in Christ Jesus. ₂₇And all who have been united with Christ in baptism have put on Christ, like putting on new clothes.
>
> ₂₈There is no longer Jew or Gentile, slave or free, male and female. For you are all one in Christ Jesus. ₂₉And now that you belong to Christ, you are the true children of Abraham. You are his heirs, and God's promise to Abraham belongs to you.

Yes, I may not be a biological child of Abraham, but in Christ, I am his child. The sworn blessings that made the difference in the life of Isaac are also speaking for me. God is under oath to keep His Word to Abraham in my life, as He did in the life of Isaac.

> ***Understanding the depth and mystery of the covenant speaking over your life is crucial so that you will not accept what is not of God.***

We are Abraham's seed. The same covenant that ensured Isaac succeeded in a time of national disaster is at work in our lives. We can lay claim to the promise given to Abraham as though he was our physical father, for God's covenant with him is at work in our lives as well. It speaks over us and guarantees that we will never be defeated in the land. It is standing as a spiritual witness, declaring that what destroys the land is not permitted to destroy us. We are different. We are exceptional cases.

Declare with boldness: ***"Because I belong to Christ, I am a true child of Abraham. I am his descendant. Every promise God made to Abraham also belongs to me."***

God is under oath, an oath He made by Himself, in His name, to ensure that every seed of Abraham conquers their enemies and possesses the land. In Christ, we are empowered as beneficiaries of the promise and oath God had with Abraham. Therefore, this year, declare in confidence that:

- The enemies that rise against you in one way will be scattered in seven ways.

- You will conquer the cities of your enemies and possess the land.

- When others are saying there's a casting down, you will be saying there's a lifting up

- You are more than a conqueror.

- As long as you stand in Christ through obedience, the difference will be evident in your life.

HOW TO ACTIVATE THE COVENANT

[19] If you are willing and obedient, you shall eat the good of the land; [20] But if you refuse and rebel, you shall be devoured by the sword"; for the mouth of the Lord has spoken - **Isaiah 1: 19-20**

Knowledge, faith, and obedience are the keys to activating the power of the covenant. Isaac knew the covenant, believed wholeheartedly in it and obeyed God. So, he prospered and ate the good of the land.

When the famine started, Isaac wanted to move out of the country, but God spoke to him and said, *"Don't go nowhere. Stay in the land."*

He did and subsequently prospered in the same year, so much that the entire nation begged him to go away because he became more powerful than them.

> *Even when an evil sword is raised over the land, obedience to God will suspend it over your life.*

May we receive grace to discern God's voice and obey at all times, in Jesus name.

If you want the covenant to speak for you, you must know the covenant. Consider what I have said in this chapter as an introduction to God's covenant with Abraham. You need to go beyond it. Find as many verses as you can and read up everything God said to and about Abraham. Then believe them and commit yourself to walk in obedience.

Your knowledge, faith, and obedience will guarantee the covenant speaks for you no matter what happens in the land.

PRAYERS/DECLARATIONS

This year, (....), I declare that I am willing to walk in obedience. Therefore, I shall be blessed and prosperous in the land. I shall eat the good of the land where I live, in Jesus name.

Through Jesus Christ, I am a seed of Abraham.

Abraham is my father, and God's covenant with him is working in my life.

When others are saying there's a casting down, I will be saying there's a lifting up.

I am supernaturally empowered to possess the gates of my enemies.

I am empowered to overcome all traps, arrows, and plans of the enemy designed against me this year.

Whoever rises against me this year (...)will not survive. They will scatter and be destroyed, in the name of Jesus Christ.

Today, in the name of Jesus Christ, I declare that no matter what happens this year, only good things will happen in my life and family.

There is a grace of difference and excellence in my life. I will be blessed in the country, blessed in the city, and blessed in the community.

The hearts of kings and men that matter will work for my good, in Jesus name.

I remind myself that I am different. I am specially, wonderfully, and fearfully made. I am not like everyone else. What stops others will not stop me because God's covenant with Abraham speaks over my life.

O Lord, equip me with everything good that I may live in Your plans this year. Help me to do Your will. Work in me to desire that which is pleasing in Your sight, in the name of Jesus Christ.

It is written that God works in us to desire and act according to His good purpose. Therefore, by the Holy Spirit and mysterious supernatural happenings of God in my life, I will desire and live in God's purpose for my life this year, in Jesus name.

Amen.

REMEMBER THIS

You may not be the biological child of Abraham, but in Christ, You are his child. The sworn blessings that made the difference in the life of Isaac are also speaking for you.

DAY 5

YOUR CASE IS DIFFERENT

Genesis 26: 12-13 - ₁₂Then Isaac sowed seed in that land and received in the same year a hundred times as much as he had planted, and the Lord favored him with blessings.

₁₃And the man became great and gained more and more until he became very wealthy and distinguished (AMPC).

Think about this. In the year that everybody was complaining, whining, and frustrated about a national crisis, one immigrant man went to his farms and planted crops. It was odd and even crazy. There was drought, death, and a nationwide problem. Everyone was protesting and waiting for some government intervention. But he went about cultivating his lands.

What did he know that others did not know? What gave him such temerity?

The covenant.

He knew that being under the covenant covering of God with his father gave him a special status. He knew that he was different. There was something at work in his life, and for him, that was not working for the general public.

> ***Today, this same mysterious force is at work in your favor. Through Christ, the same covenant is speaking over your life.***

You are a seed of Abraham, a covenant child. There are powers working in your favor that is not working for the general populace. Accept this revelation without sentiments and declare your difference.

"But Daniel," you say, "I've had a lot of problems in my life and so many unanswered prayers. How can you say there is something special about me? I'm suffering."

Well, first, you're not alone in these thoughts. There are times I've asked myself, "If God is with me, why do I have these setbacks? Why does it seem as though the enemy is pushing so hard without any help?"

One day, though, while meditating, the Holy Spirit said to me: *"Just because you've had many problems in life does not mean you're no longer who God made you to be. You're who God says you are regardless of your problems and challenges."*

The first thing God wants you to do this year is to recognize who you are in Him. Recognize that He is at work in your life and that you are unique. You are a covenant child.

You're not some poor, helpless soul just trying to survive and make ends meet. You're not some defeated church fanatic destined to die without hope.

On the contrary, you are a rare innovation by the Almighty God. You are fearfully and wonderfully made. There's something special about you that is not in anyone else.

> *Your challenges and problems are not a picture of how wretched your life is or how your life should be.*

Yesterday, while in fellowship, God spoke to me and said, "The challenges in your life are not because you're under a curse, but because God is bringing out the best in you. As a gold, you're being refined. You're getting better."

To get started on the right path this year, God says you should declare who you are and the blessing (covenant) at work in your life. Declare the forces supernaturally released in your favor, not the forces working against you.

You're not a loser. You're a covenant child.

> ***You may have lost some battles, but that doesn't mean you're a loser.***

Isaac sweated it out; he also lost some wells. But when everything was said and brought to book, he excelled more than everyone.

This year, when all is said and done, it will be recorded that you won.

As I said earlier, don't look at yourself and look at your problems and begin to wonder if what God is saying is true. God's word is true regardless of the difficulties we face.

If you don't know who you are in God and what God says about you and accept it with all your heart, you will be a victim of the circumstances in the world.

So, today, invest yourself in scriptures, read up as much as possible, and appropriate everything God says you are. Then declare them by faith and pray that this consciousness never departs from you.

Even if the world falls upside down, what God says you are is what you are. Nothing changes God's words about your life.

PRAYERS/DECLARATIONS

Heavenly Father,

I pray that through the Holy Spirit, You will show me who I am in You through Christ. Show me the mysteries and forces working for and in my favor.

Show me every blessing that I do not currently appropriate into my life and destiny.

Guide my study, reading and search and enlighten my mind.

Help me to accept my position in You and not the voice of my past and the challenges of my present, in Jesus name.

Today, according to the Word of God, I boldly declare that....I am made in God's image.

I resemble God.

I have the nature of God.

I think like God, create like God, and excel like Him.

Through Christ, I am restored to God's original plans for my life.

I am a child of Abraham, and the covenant of Abraham is at work in my life.

This year, I will be favored every day of my life.

Because I am covered in God's covenant, everything will fall for me in pleasant places.

When others complain, God's grace and mystery will be at work in my life, causing me to testify.

I will prevail in all circumstances this year.

I have authority, and I rule over the powers of the air, the land, and the sea.

Principalities, powers, thrones, familiar spirits, witches, and wizards bow before me and tremble at my appearance and commands. I rule over them and overthrow their plans.

This year, nothing shall, by any means, hurt me, in Jesus name.

I am a new creation in Christ; my old life has passed away; I now live a new life.

I cannot be judged, accused, and condemned because of my past errors, mistakes, failures, and sins.

In Christ, I am righteous before God. All of my sins have been forgiven. They are no more in existence.

I am redeemed, sanctified, justified, and made holy before God.

I am free from the law of sin and death.

I'm out of darkness and now in the Kingdom of Light, where Jesus is the head.

I am seated with Christ in the heavenly places far about principalities and powers, thrones and dominions.

I now reign with Christ

The life I live today, I live through Christ.

I am filled with the Spirit of love, of power, and of a sound mind.

Anxiety, depression, fear, and all forms of oppression of the mind are far from me.

No weapon fashioned against me and my household shall prosper, and every tongue that rises against us stands condemned, in Jesus name.

I am born of God.

The Holy Spirit is in me.

I am not a slave to the flesh.

My spirit is in tune with the Holy Spirit.

I do not live in sin.

*I am protected from all forms of temptations
that lead to error and sin, in Jesus name*

---

*I have the mind of Christ, and I shall succeed in
everything I lay my hands to do.*

*As nothing could stop Jesus until He finished his
course, so will nothing be able to withstand or
stop me this year.*

*God's wisdom flows through me, making me an
agent of peace, salvation, kindness, and
solution to others.*

This year, I shall be the head and not the tail.

I shall lend and not borrow.

I shall not live in debt.

I declare every debt in my life and family supernaturally canceled, in Jesus name.

Henceforth, I shall sow and harvest.

My givings, seeds of faith, and offerings of the past are coming back into my life as harvests of breakthroughs and testimonies this year.

I shall have an abundance of opportunities.

I will never be out of a job and income.

Through the Spirit of wisdom and revelation in the knowledge of Jesus, the eyes of my heart will always be enlightened so that I always know what to do and know the hope I have in Christ.

I shall never be stranded again.

Throughout this year, I and everyone in my family will have peace, the peace of God that passes all understanding.

The Spirit of God in me is greater than the enemy, the devil, and his demons, in the world.

Evil shall not come near our dwelling.

God's light is shining brighter and brighter in and around us. His protection is with us. He is with us as a pillar of fire by night and a pillar of cloud by day.

Violence, robbery, pestilences, and all forms of terrors are far from us this year, in Jesus name.

This year, I shall rule in every aspect of my life because:

- *I have received abundant grace and the gift of righteousness and reign in life through Jesus Christ.*

- *I have received the power of the Holy Spirit, and He is the Spirit of wisdom, power, and Mighty acts.*

- *Through me, the Holy Spirit will do great miracles of healings, deliverance, salvation, and restoration in my life, family, Church, and community, in Jesus name*

This year, I flow in God's grace and love, even as Christ loved.

I curse the spirit of fear, hatred, bitterness, anger, quarreling, and resentment and declare that they have no place in my life.

I curse every form of harmful addiction, connection, relationship, and soul tie and declare that I shall not be a victim.

Yes, I will not be a victim of wrong connections, associations, and attachments.

This year, I will only connect with the right people ordained by God for my destiny and purpose, in Jesus name.

This year, God supplies all of my needs according to His riches in glory by Christ Jesus.

I declare that I am rich in mercy, forgiveness, kindness, love, discernment, and spiritual insights.

I receive grace to love, to give, and to bless.

As I do, God's blesses my life and causes others to love, to give, and to bless me in good measure, pressed down and running over the extent I give, in Jesus name

---

I am God's workmanship, created in Christ to do good works that He has prepared for me before the foundation of this world.

This year, God will cause me both to will and to do His good pleasure.

In all situations, I live by faith, not by sight.

I am renewed day by day until the perfect day, in the name of Jesus Christ.

As I hear God's Word, my heart receives instruction on specific things to do to excel this year. And as I do as the Word says, I will be blessed, always.

I declare that:

- *I am a joint-heir with Christ (Romans 8:17).*

- *I am more than a conqueror through Christ who loves me (Romans 8:37).*

- *I overcome the devil, the enemy of my soul and his agents, by the blood of Jesus Christ and the word of my testimony (Rev. 12:11).*

- *I have everything I need to live a godly life, and I am fortified in God's divine nature (2 Peter 1:3-4).*

- *I am an ambassador for Christ, with the full benefits of Heaven backing me. I have honor, respect, and dignity in everything, and everywhere I go (2 Cor. 5:20).*

- *I am a chosen generation, a royal priesthood, a holy nation, purchased by the Blood of Jesus Christ (1 Peter 2:9).*

- *Through Christ, I am the righteousness of God. I have the right standing with Him. (2 Corinthians 5:21).*

- *My body is a temple of the Holy Spirit; through Him, I humbly surrender to God every day, and the devil flees from me (1 Corinthians 6:19).*

- *I am the light of the world; I shine every day, even if there is thick darkness attacking the world (Matthew 5:14).*

- *I have been redeemed and forgiven of all my sins. I am made clean through the blood of Jesus Christ. I will not let anyone or the devil accuse me of my past anymore.*

- *I have been delivered from the community and the power of darkness and brought into God's Community and kingdom. Today, Jesus Christ is my Lord and Savior, and He is my King. No other power controls my life, family, and destiny*

- *The Blood of Jesus Christ has redeemed me from the curse of sin, sickness, and poverty.*

- *My faith and life are rooted in Christ. I bear fruits of joy and thanksgiving every day.*

- *I am healed and made whole in Christ Jesus. I am walking in divine health every day, all the days of my life. Sicknesses and diseases are defeated and will no longer reign in my spirit, soul, and body, in Jesus name.*

- *God loves me because He loves me. His love remains with me every day, throughout the year, and throughout my life. His love renews and strengthens me day by day and empowers me to press on to fulfill His plan for my life, in Jesus name.*

Today, Lord, I throw away the cloak of laziness.

I surrender the coat of low self-esteem and self-pity.

I give up the cover of excuses and fear.

And I put on the shield of faith and take on the mantle of purpose.

I speak to myself this day and declare: no more will I sit in darkness.

I arise from now onwards and connect to God's purpose for my life. I arise and connect to God's mercy and help.

I arise and receive boldness to take every divine step ordained for my success this year.

May every spirit of carelessness, negligence, and negative self-focus cease to exist in my life.

May pride, arrogance, and self-dependence end in my life today.

May all forms of evil thoughts, imaginations, and destructive strongholds wither from my spirit today.

It is written that while men slept, the enemy came and sowed tares.

Heavenly Father, I pray this day that the Holy Spirit will wake me up from all forms of slumber.

Whatever the enemy has planted in my life and family, in the past, as a result of my spiritual sleepiness, Lord, let them be uprooted and destroyed this day, in Jesus name.

Father Lord, open my eyes to see and understand what the enemy has broken in my life, career, family, and ministry; and help me in this season of waiting on You to demand Your total restoration.

Anything that makes me powerless in the spirit world, Lord Jesus Christ, take it out of my life today.

Every door I have opened out of ignorance, fear, or doubt; everything that has enabled the devil to harass my life and family before now, I cancel them, in Jesus name.

This is my year of Rehoboth. I am empowered to excel; I am certified to shine no matter the situation in the world, in Jesus name.

Amen.

REMEMBER THIS…

You are a seed of Abraham, a covenant child. There are some forces working in your favor that is not working for the general populace. Accept this revelation without sentiments and declare your difference.

DAY 6

WALK BY FAITH, NOT BY SIGHT

Genesis 26: 12-13 - ₁₂Then Isaac sowed seed in that land and received in the same year a hundred times as much as he had planted, and the Lord favored him with blessings.

₁₃And the man became great and gained more and more until he became very wealthy and distinguished (AMPC).

So, now, we agree that the covenant was a powerful spiritual force in the life of Isaac. Knowing that he was a covenant son empowered his boldness to think differently. He refused to accept the negative national story because he knew he was special.

In the same way, thinking *covenantly* and differently is the way to have a different outcome in the world we live in. It is the key to being preserved and exempted from the calamities that bedevil the world year in year out.

> *You are not the same as everyone else. There is a powerful force at work in your life that is not at work for the general populace. This force is the covenant. Think highly of it.*

Because you are in God's covenant, there is a sworn blessing over your life. Even when the wickedness in the world causes others to say there's a casting down, you will be saying there's a lifting up.

In the same year of famine, there was also abundance. In the same year of travails, there was also comfort. But the abundance and ease were not for everyone else. It was for those under covenant with God.

God says that you will walk in abundance amid famine. You will have comfort amid travails. You will be lifted even in times of meltdown. Why?

Because you are a covenant child.

Think differently; think *covenantly*.

You are special. Your case is different.

> **Think about your spiritual connection more than you worry about the problems in the world.**

Declare this again and again:

"I am in God's covenant.

"The covenant is a shield against the works of the enemy.

"I am divinely exempted from the evils in the world, in Jesus name."

WALK BY FAITH, NOT BY SIGHT

I have written many articles on faith and recently published two books on faith: Ignite and Roar. And for me, faith makes the difference between manifestation and condemnation. Without faith, nothing else works. Without faith, we will not be healed, we will not propser, and we will not succeed.

> *If we don't walk by faith, we will suffer the same torments the world suffers.*

Underline that statement. Repeat it to yourself, now, and as many times as you can. That is God speaking to you right there.

Without faith, we will suffer the same tortures others are suffering.

Did you get that?

Imagine this: God told Isaac, "Hey! Stay in this land. There's a covenant over your life. I will bless you."

Isaac said, "Yes, sir."

And stayed in the land.

But notice what he did next. He began to acquire lands for farming.

I didn't read anywhere that God told him to do that. God didn't say, *"Okay, now, go and buy lands. Go and get corn seeds. Go and do this; go and do that."*

Isaac did the rest on his own - by his faith.

By his faith, he moved on to buy lands. By his faith, he moved on to getting seeds to plant. And by his faith, he determined how to water the crops he cultivated.

The residents must have sold the lands to him at very moderate rates. They must have considered that the man was crazy to buy farming lands in the middle of a drought, mass deaths, and national crisis. They must have wondered what kind of ignorant refugee he was.

But he went on.

And he didn't just negotiate and buy lands. He recruited staff, trained them, found seeds, planted them, and sought water to water them. All of this, in the same year, that there was a national drought and setback.

That was walking by faith and not by sight.

Behold the proud, his soul is not upright in him; but the just shall live by his faith - Habakkuk 2:4

Beloved, we are in God's covenant. We are the children of Abraham. The covenant is a powerful force speaking for and over our lives. However, without faith, we will not see the manifestation of the blessings of the covenant.

Being in the covenant does not equal God coddling us. No. God may not tell your neighbors to hand over their lands to you free of charge. You might have to approach the sellers and make an offer. You might have to approach a lending company and tell them the terms you want.

The covenant does not mean the doctors will never tell you something bad. They will read out their diagnosis and, sometimes, it won't sound good. But you will have to look up the *Word* about your health and stick with what it says, and walk by faith, not by sight.

God won't cook our food, submit our CVs, and attend job interviews for us. He will not advertise our companies, recruit our staff, train them, empower them, and negotiate with our suppliers. He will give us wisdom, but we will have to put in the necessary efforts.

Being in the covenant does not mean that we will not see the problems in the country, neither does it mean we will hear God's voice from the sky every morning, saying, *"Hey, go greet Mr Shane and tell him to give you a thousand bucks."*

We will see the problems happening around, but we must know that we are empowered by the covenant to overcome. Then we must walk by faith, not by sight. Otherwise, we will become victims of what is happening to everyone.

In other words, even if you see deaths and crises, you must say and keep on saying, "I shall not die. I shall not lack. God is with me."

Then you must put your faith to work. You must do your part even if it doesn't make sense. Then God will be right there to protect, preserve and bless your actions of faith

SENSE VS. FAITH

Think about our father, Abraham. The covenant we are declaring today was activated and established by faith. The scripture says, *"By faith,*

Abraham obeyed when he was called to go out to the place he would receive as an inheritance. And he went out, not knowing where he was going" (Heb. 11:8).

Imagine that when God spoke to Abraham, he began to think about the geographical technicalities. Imagine that he waited to see proofs first before taking the first steps and leaving his comfort zone. We will not be where we are today, nor will we be talking about the covenant of Abraham.

But by faith, he moved out of his birthplace, traveling through unknown areas to establish a new country. He didn't have a child, neither did he know where he was going. He only heard God and started his journey.

Imagine him discussing with his friends:

Abraham: "Hey guys, I'll be leaving town tomorrow.

His Friends: "Where are you going?

Abraham: "I don't know yet.

His Friends: "What are you saying? What do you mean you don't know where you're going?

Abraham: "Well, I don't know where I am going. But I am leaving tomorrow.

His Friends: "Hmmm! Okay, so, what are you going to do in this unknown place?

Abraham: "I'm going to establish a new nation that will be strong and great on the earth.

His Friends: *(Laughter).* "What is wrong with you, Abe? You don't even have a child, and you're seventy-five. What's messing with your mind?

Abraham: "God spoke to me a few days ago in a dream. I'll be leaving tomorrow.

His Friends: "Dream? ?????"

If Abraham were the older brother of some of us, we would call a family meeting for him. First, we will contact the family doctor and tell him that our brother is mentally unstable. We will say his age and childlessness are affecting his reasoning. Then we will consult the elders of the land to try and talk some sense into him.

How can a seventy-five-year-old brother wake up one morning and say he had a dream, and boom, he is leaving his homeland to go and establish a new country? What kind of madness was that? And to think that he doesn't even have a child. His wife was barren, and he refused to marry a second wife. How was he going to start the new nation? This was too much of a mental breakdown to condone.

But you know what? He was acting in faith.

Faith is acting on the Word of God even when you're unsure of what the physical results would be. It is taking action based on something God says or something He is saying in your heart, even if it's not making sense.

> *Faith doesn't always have to make sense. That's why it's faith. If it always makes complete sense before you do it, it's not faith.*

This year, God says, "Walk by faith, not by sight. That's how to excel in the famine. That's how to have comfort even in the travails. That's how to stay in supply even in the hardship."

Don't get carried away by any event or situation that arises in your life or in the world. Instead, pay attention in your heart. At every needed time, God will drop the right word, a word in season, in your heart. The word may not come from the sky or with some charismatic shakings. It may not come from some special prophet.

On the contrary, the word may come while you're reading a book or listening to a sermon. It may come while you're meditating or singing.

> *If you make your heart ready and prepared, you will never lack the right word to lead you every time*

And when God gives you a word, you will know. If it's something He wants you to do, it will give you peace, joy, and assurance. If it's something He doesn't want you to do, it will make you uneasy, uncomfortable, and restless.

Whenever you sense a word from God in your heart, get up and follow His leading. Don't wait for everything to be okay. Faith is acting on a word from God, and that is the key to abundance in the famine.

PRAYERS/DECLARATIONS

Today, I decree that all things are possible for me. I can do all things through Christ, who gives me strength.

From now onwards, I give up all forms of unbelief stopping me from acting on the Word of God for my protection, health, and breakthrough.

I decree that I am not under any evil oppression anymore. I am living in the Light, where darkness has no say.

This year, Father, open my heart to receive more of You daily. Keep me continually hungry and thirsty for more of Your Word. Grant that my heart will remain fertile for the entrance of Thy Word and that my life will bring forth the fruits of faith, in the name of Jesus Christ.

From today, I command all my sense calculations and reasonings to give way to faith in God's Word. I declare that my obedience and response to God's revealed Word will be swift and perfect, in Jesus name.

I declare my unwavering faith in the power of God's Word. I believe in God's promises for my life. I know that God is faithful who has promised, and His promises are Yea and Amen.

I re-commit myself to be invested in God's promises and to hold onto them no matter what is happening in the physical, for I know that He that has promised is faithful.

This year, victory is mine every day, in Jesus name.

Amen.

REMEMBER THIS

Don't get carried away by any event or situation that arises in your life or in the world. Instead, pay attention in your heart. At every needed time, God will drop the right word, a word in season, in your heart.

DAY 7

ALREADY EMPOWERED

₁₂ Then Isaac sowed in that land and reaped in the same year a hundredfold, and the Lord blessed him.

₁₃ The man began to prosper and continued prospering until he became very prosperous; ₁₄ for he had possessions of flocks and possessions of herds and a great number of servants. So the Philistines envied him. – Gen. 26: 12-13

One of the most powerful revelations that God enshrined in my heart in 2021 is this: "God will never ask you to do something He has not already empowered you to do... If God is asking something from you, it's because He has already given it to you."

God only asked Abraham to sacrifice Isaac after Isaac came, not before he was born.

If there is something God is laying in your heart to do, you can do it. You may look at the economy, look at your problems, and come up with excuses. But if God says you can, then you can.

In 1998, at the age of 21, God laid it in my heart to write whatever message He gave me. He said to me, "A time will come when they will bless the world and set the captives free."

I was young, untrained, unexposed, and unrefined then. But I kept writing from that time. Of course, I didn't know how my books would reach people beyond my immediate environment. There was nothing to think that writing would be a big deal for my life and ministry. But I kept on.

Today, our book ministry is one of the most successful aspects of our work. Thousands of people access our books every month and are changed inside out by the messages we share.

Beloved, if you cannot do it, God would not have said it to you. You have what it takes to be and do what God wants you to be and do. Just stop looking outside and start looking deeper and deeper inside.

In childbearing, for instance, what produces a child is already in the man and the woman. You do not have to buy, borrow, or re-invent it. God already put it there.

When God says in the scriptures, "Be fruitful and multiply," He is also saying, *"I have empowered you to bear fruits. You already have everything you will ever need."*

God will never ask you to do something He hasn't already empowered you with the ability to do.

So, if you say, "But God, there are many trials in the world. Things are messed up. I don't even have a job, and I'm very sick. People are dying everywhere, and the economy is terrible."

God will look at you and say, *"What are you talking about? I know there are problems in the world. I see, and I know about the darkness and the famine. However, I want you to go and do what I want you to do. I want you to grow, bear fruits and multiply. You're in charge and unstoppable."*

I believe that Isaac argued with himself, prayed, and tried to convince God that planting seeds during famine did not make sense. Where would he get water to water the crops? How would he deal with pests? How would he deal with mockery from the community? What about taxes and government policies? After all, he was just a stranger in the land.

There were many genuine reasons not to plant crops in the land or expect too much that year. But with God's prodding, he went ahead. Though the fears and issues were there, he moved on. And God honored his actions of faith.

The good part is that he did not need any exceptional external resources to make the kind of progress he made that year. God already provided everything, and they were already right there with him.

> Ephesians 1:3-4 - Blessed and worthy of praise be the God and Father of our Lord Jesus Christ, **who has blessed us with every spiritual blessing in the heavenly realms in Christ**, just as in His love He chose us in Christ before the foundation of the world so that we would be holy - that is, consecrated, set apart for Him, purpose-driven - and blameless in His sight" (AMP).

Beloved, everything is already provided. You are already empowered. You are already vested with every resource you need for growth and increase. You are already authorized for Rehoboth.

Stop calculating what you don't have, and ask God to show and connect you with the abundance of resources already available to you. You will be amazed at what you will discover if you believe.

I agree that you got problems here and there. But your problems do not cancel what God has done in your life or said about you. You are already empowered to prosper and excel.

> ***You're empowered and blessed because God says so, not because of the amount you have in the bank.***

The covenant is more important and more powerful than the problems in your life and the ones in the world.

Rest in the Lord. Stop crying and begging for things as though you're disadvantaged. Start speaking authoritatively and command your desires to come forth - in faith, not in fear.

Shout it: "I am abundantly blessed in Christ."

You're already empowered. Believe and receive the word and walk by faith, not by sight. You will be fruitful even in the famine.

WHAT FRUITS?

What fruits does God expect in abundance from you this year?

- The fruit of the Holy Spirit: love, joy, peace, kindness, patience, temperance, faithfulness, and gentleness.

- The fruit of righteous living

- The fruit of excellence in business, ministry, and career

- The fruit of expansion in the works of your hands. You will never be out of a job.

- The fruit of excellent relationships

- The fruit of good health, prosperity, and unstoppable breakthrough.

- The fruit of the womb

- The fruit of your barns, and so on

God wants you to be fruitful in every area of your life – spiritually and physically. He knows that there will be evil and challenges in the world. But He has empowered you to overcome and still bear fruits. Accept this spiritual reality for your life.

PRAYERS/DECLARATIONS

Heavenly Father,

I thank You for blessing me with all spiritual blessings in Christ Jesus. I thank You that I am already blessed, empowered, and enriched.

I am not struggling to be blessed.

I am already blessed.

I have every resource, capital, and help I need to grow and excel.

I am blessed and empowered, notwithstanding what I am seeing or not seeing today.

Father, uproot all forms of unbelief from my heart today.

I know that there are many times that my faith is weak, when I want to see before believing.

But today, Lord, I repent and rest in Your Word.

This year, help me remember that I am already empowered to bear fruits.

Help me always to remember that my case is different.

Help me to align myself to Your words for my life, and not with the events in the world, in Jesus name.

I declare that through Christ, I am a child of Abraham. God's covenant with Abraham is also working in my favor. The same grace, grit, and wisdom in the life of Isaac are in my life. My efforts and seeds this year will be abundantly blessed, and I will see hundredfold returns in all that I do, in Jesus name.

O Lord, I surrender my fears and worries to You and accept Your Word for my life.

I declare that everything You have said concerning me is undoubtedly coming to pass.

This year, I will excel because I am different.

I am special.

I am fortified and blessed.

Only good things will happen in my life and family.

I will walk by faith and not by sight.

I will not let what I see and what I don't see determine what I believe about God and about myself, in Jesus name.

I will bear fruits of righteousness.

I will see an increase in my finances.

I will have an abundance of business and career opportunities.

I will have an abundance of supernatural ideas to grow and increase in all areas of my life.

I will bear fruits of the spirit.

My life will be a model and an example for others.

I will never be stranded or stagnant, no matter what. The covenant speaking for me forbids stagnation and failure, in Jesus name.

Amen.

REMEMBER THIS

If there is something God is laying in your heart to do, you can do it. You may look at the economy and look at your problems and come up with excuses. But if God says you can do it or become it, then you can do it and become it.

DAY 8

STAY CONNECTED

₁I am the true vine, and my Father is the gardener. ₂He cuts off every branch in me that bears no fruit, while every branch that does bear fruit he prunes so that it will be even more fruitful.

₃You are already clean because of the word I have spoken to you. ₄**Remain in me, as I also remain in you. No branch can bear fruit by itself; it must remain in the vine. Neither can you bear fruit unless you remain in me.**

₅"I am the vine; you are the branches. If you remain in me and I in you, you will bear much fruit; apart from me, you can do nothing.

₆If you do not remain in me, you are like a branch that is thrown away and withers; such branches are picked up, thrown into the fire, and burned.

₇If you remain in me and my words remain in you, ask whatever you wish, and it will be done for you.

₈This is to my Father's glory, that you bear much fruit, showing yourselves to be my disciples – John 15:1-8

In this passage, Jesus gives us the key to bearing fruits. He says, *"Remain in me, as I also remain in you. No branch can bear fruit by itself; it must remain in the vine. Neither can you bear fruit unless you remain in me."*

Jesus didn't say that the state of the economy determines our fruitfulness. Neither did He say that what people are saying against you will determine your productivity. He said that our fruitfulness and productivity is determined by our remaining in him.

The plans and secret meetings of ten thousand witches and wizards do not matter. As long as we remain in Him, we will be fruitful and productive. As long as we remain in Him, we will not suffer drought – spiritually and physically.

So how do we remain in Him?

By staying in the Word.

Jesus is the Word of God. So, when He says, "Remain in me, and I will remain in you," He means, *"Stay in the Word, and the Word will stay in you."* As long as the Word stays in you, you will be fruitful.

As long as Isaac focused his mind on the Word of God and the power of God, he was empowered to be fruitful, irrespective of what happened in the land. The word in him pushed back the enemies' powers and kept him stayed on even in the hostile times.

Thank God it's easier today compared to the times of Isaac. Today, we have the Bible in its complete form. We have books helping us to digest the Bible. We have preachers, YouTube, and daily broadcasts. The Word is more accessible these days compared to the times of Isaac.

All Isaac had was one dream from God and a self-reminder of what his father had said about God. He held on to those words and prevailed.

Today, we are blessed that the Word is available in every corner. All you have to do is go for the WORD that builds up your faith and teaches you how to be better.

> *Stay on the word; focus on the Word every day; stay on it until you dream it, breathe it, and it becomes your involuntary response in every situation.*

As long as you hold onto the Word in all things, you will prevail in all things. You will have comfort no matter the struggles, and you will shine no matter the darkness.

The seed that produces the fruit of the Holy Spirit, the fruits of righteousness, the fruits of good health, and financial prosperity is the Word of God.

You must make a conscious effort to dwell on the Word more than ever, and your profiting will appear to all. The Word will correct you, empower you, restore you, guide you, and give you wisdom on what to do every time.

> *The more of God's word you have in you, the sharper your spiritual sword will be, and the easier it will be to put out the fiery darts of the enemy.*

The more of the Word you have, the more of the Holy Spirit's power you will display, and the more you will push back the forces of darkness and let your light shine.

Tell yourself: "I will be fruitful this year, for I will dwell on the Word. I will hear God's voice; I will obey, and I will prevail against all odds."

PRAYERS/DECLARATIONS

Heavenly Father,

Thank You because it is Your will for me to be fruitful, to prevail, and to multiply this year. Thank You because my time of supernatural expansion, growth, multiplication, and fruitfulness is now, and You have already empowered me with what I need to be fruitful.

I pray today, Lord, by the Holy Spirit, cause me to dwell in Your Word and cause the Word to live in me. I know that Jesus is the Word. As I stay in the Word, Jesus dwells in me and causes me to prosper and bear fruits that abound.

Holy Spirit, grant me access to Your light. As I read, study, and listen to Your Word, give me specific instructions about my personal life, relationships, career, health, and finances.

Show me specific things I need to do to bring about the changes and miracles You plan for me this year, in Jesus name.

This year, O Lord, instruct me and teach me in the way that I should go. Guide me with Thine eye. I do not want to be like the horse or the mule, which has no understanding, which must be harnessed with bit and bridle to stay on track.

Open my ears to hear; open my eyes to see, and open my heart to understand the path You have ordained for me this year and what I must do to walk in the liberty and power that I have through Jesus Christ, in Jesus name.

Today, O Lord, I curse the spirit of barrenness; I curse the spirit of unfruitfulness; whatever causes me to remain at one spot and unfruitful,

I command them to be destroyed by fire, in the name of Jesus Christ.

I pull down every stronghold, evil thought, imagination, character, habit, or relationship that fights against my abundance and prosperity.

I curse every witch, wizard, or agent of darkness working hard to make me remain at one spot, fearful and unfruitful.

I command to end every plan working against my productiveness, fruitfulness, and growth, in Jesus name.

May every hidden spiritual seed planted in my spirit, soul, and body, preventing me from living a life of faith and walking in God's shoes for my life, be uprooted from this day on, in Jesus name.

I declare that the blessings of God are upon my life. I shall prevail; I shall see supernatural growth and fruitfulness in my life this year, in Jesus name I pray.

Amen.

REMEMBER THIS

The plans and secret meetings of ten thousand witches and wizards do not matter. As long as we remain in Christ, we will be fruitful. As long as we remain in Him, we will not suffer drought – spiritually and physically.

DAY 9

HEARING GOD'S VOICE EVERY DAY

Genesis 26: 1-6 – ₁There was a famine in the land, besides the first famine that was in the days of Abraham. And Isaac went to Abimelech king of the Philistines, in Gerar.

₂Then the Lord appeared to him and said:

"Do not go down to Egypt; live in the land of which I shall tell you. ₃Dwell in this land, and I will be with you and bless you; for to you and your descendants I give all these lands, and I will perform the oath which I swore to Abraham, your father. ₄And I will make your descendants multiply as the stars of heaven; I will give to your descendants all these lands; and in your seed, all the nations of the earth shall be blessed; ₅because Abraham obeyed My voice and kept My charge, My commandments, My statutes, and My laws."

₆So Isaac dwelt in Gerar.

For years, I heard teachings on "Isaac sowed in the land in the same year and reaped a hundredfold." They were usually fascinating, especially when the preachers used them to preach on giving. I never argue with the Word. I believe that everyone comes from the angle of their revelation.

However, over the years, I've learned to *"read the full story to get the full message."*

In other words, to know how to get the results of *"a hundred times as much as he had planted, and the Lord favored him with blessings,"* we need to know what he did. Don't just focus on the glory without a thought to the process.

And one of the keys to this blessing is hearing His voice and walking in obedience. The moment the famine began, Isaac started making plans to leave the country and *go down* to Egypt. But he had a dream, and God said to him, "Stay in the land. Don't leave."

He obeyed. And that was the foundation of every other thing that happened with him in the land.

In other words, *hearing God's voice was the basis for experiencing the blessings in the famine.*

If Isaac had left the country, he'd probably return in that same year, but not with a hundredfold increase in his labor. He may have been like Naomi, who said, "I traveled out full but came back empty."

Now, if you read and compare Isaac's story and Naomi's, they had some similarities in the beginning but ended differently. While Isaac listened to the voice of God and stayed back during the famine, Elimelech, the husband of Naomi, traveled out with his family (for greener pastures) without listening to the voice of God during the famine. Eventually, Isaac was blessed, while Elimelech put his family in great anguish.

Same events. Different outcomes. Why?

Listening and not listening.

> **As Christians, we are not to be led by problems and challenges but by the Holy Spirit.**

If you let circumstances decide your actions of what to do, what not to do, and where to go, you will not enjoy the full blessings designed for your life.

DELIVERANCE FROM YOUR WAYS

Proverbs 14:12 - There is a way which seems right to a man and appears straight before him, but at the end of it is the way of death (AMPC)

"O God, deliver me from my own ways" is a prayer we must pray every morning, all the days of our lives. Why? Because one wrong decision, one wrong move, one bad relationship or connection can set us back for many years.

We live in a wicked world. Apart from demonic spirits trying to stop us, there are also very subtle, hostile, witchcraft-minded individuals around us, waiting for us to make one mistake so that they can devour us.

Always ask God to deliver you from your own ways, plans, ideas, and connections, which may seem right in your eyes, but which may end up a trap.

> ***God's continual guidance is the key to pushing back the enemies into oblivion and walking in victory every day.***

Thankfully, God's leading is not a mystery. He is always leading and guiding us. All we need to do is come to Him, believing and trusting to receive His guidance.

DESIRE HIS VOICE, NOT JUST HIS BLESSINGS

This year, desire His voice like never before. Don't just seek His blessings on your plans; pursue His plans for His blessings. And when He leads, follow. That's how to excel in the travails.

"But Daniel," you say, "I love to hear God's voice. But He's not talking to me. How do I hear His voice? And how will I be sure that the voice I'm hearing is His voice?"

This is the question I get asked all the time. It's also a question that I ask too. But one thing I've learned over the years is that God is always speaking to us. Most times, though, He speaks to us in certain ways while we want Him to talk to us in other ways.

In other words, we are the ones not listening. We want God to talk to us in unfamiliar ways instead of listening to Him.

For instance, many people want to hear God speak to them through audible voices, open visions, or angelic visitations. Others want someone to come to them and say, "Hey, your name is Susan. Three days from now, you plan to travel to Germany. God says you should not go."

God can certainly speak to us in these ways. The problem is that we must not want Him to talk to us in those ways that we fail to listen to Him speaking to us in other ways.

It is not in our place to insist we must hear His voice through open visions, trances, or angelic encounters. Ours is to surrender to Him and listen to Him through His Word. His Word is the primary way He is speaking to us. As we surrender and listen to Him through His Word and the inward witness, over time, we will begin to have deeper and deeper encounters.

The Word is as powerful as other methods of His direction and leading. For instance, I desperately wanted to be sure God was involved in some things we were involved in recently. I prayed over and over and didn't hear a voice, so to say. I waited, meditated, and read the Bible. Yet I didn't get that assurance that I've heard from Him.

Then I started listening to a particular preacher that I've not been listening to all these years. I'm convinced now that God led me to start listening to this man of God. As I listened to him, every question in my heart was answered. No, he didn't prophesy to me. It was recorded messages, so he couldn't have known me to prophecy to me. But his messages touched on many of my questions, and I knew what God wanted me to do about what we were doing.

THE WORD IS A LAMP

The easiest way to hear the voice of God is through His Word. We access light through the Word, for the Bible says:

Your word is a lamp for my feet, a light on my path - Psalm 119:105.

As you read the scriptures, meditate on the Word, or hear a teaching or preaching, desire and look for the light in the Word and not just the stories. In your spirit, the light will come. You will suddenly see something about what you're praying about, and you will know what to say or do.

> *Follow the direction God gives you through the Word. It's as powerful as directions received other ways.*

Some of the breakthroughs and successes I have experienced in life came through a revelation I saw through the Word. While on the Word, I could see what I must do in my spirit. After that, I got up and followed it up with action. Then I saw great results and miracles.

The light that comes through the Word shatters every form of darkness and opens tremendous doors. That light will cause you to overcome the powers of the devil and prevail in the land. It will cause you to be fruitful in famine.

BUILD YOUR FAITH WITH THE WORD

Faith comes by listening continually to God's word. Fear and unbelief also come by listening continually to something other than the Word.

> **Rom. 10:17** - So, then faith comes by hearing and hearing by the word of God.

That means that when we hear God's Word, it brings us an assurance of the truth. Our hearts are guided into what is true and what is false.

Hearing the Word of God, not the words of men, not the news, not social media, is the only way to strengthen your faith and keep yourself safe, strong, and sound, no matter the challenges in the world.

So, if you want your faith to grow, desire God's Word every day. As you read the Bible, hear messages, or listen to recordings, meditate, and listen to the revelations it drops in your heart. This is the type of hearing you need to run your race with the certainty of success every day.

PRAYERS/DECLARATIONS

Heavenly Father,

I pray today, by the Holy Spirit, grant me access to Your instruction.

As I read, study and listen to Your Word henceforth, speak to me clearly and guide me.

Instruct me and teach me how I should go and guide me with Thine eye.

Open my ears to hear; open my eyes to see, and open my heart to understand the path You ordained for me this year and what I must do to be in Your will always

---

O Lord, If there is any instruction, direction, and guidance that I have ignored in the past, knowingly or unknowingly, which is now responsible for my being spoiled, plundered, and trapped in holes; O Lord, please forgive me, and restore whatever the enemy has tampered in my life and destiny, in Jesus name

---

Henceforth, Father, I surrender to You completely. Guide me through thy Holy Spirit to remember everything You have said to me in the past that I need to obey. Teach me how to receive answers to my prayers and have victory over the circumstances confronting me, in Jesus name.

From now onwards, satan, I reject your distractions. I reject your lies and confusion in my mind.

I bind you and command all your attacks and projections targeted at blinding me towards God's voice to be destroyed, in Jesus name.

Father, Lord, inspire me with the right thoughts, ideas, and imaginations that will bring clarity to what You are leading me to do.

Connect me with the right persons through which what You are telling me will be confirmed and ascertained, in Jesus name.

In the name of Jesus Christ, I decree today that the LORD orders my paths.

I am walking in His direction for my life.

I am taking back whatever has been stolen from me in the past.

By the Holy Spirit's revelation, I will know what I should do over the following situations:

(mention specific issues you need clarity on)

And I receive grace to obey, in Jesus name.

Lord, I pray, this year, even when I plan my ways in my heart, please direct my steps in Your will, and bring glory to Your Name through my life. For it is written that a man's heart may plan his way, but You Lord directs his steps (Proverbs 16:9).

COMMIT YOUR PLANS TO THE LORD

Thank You, Lord, for the Holy Spirit who guides us into all truth and brings to us all things You have said unto us.

O Lord, I commit my plans this year into Your hands. Remove from me every idea, project, or desire, which is not of You.

Make known to me the things You have ordained for me to achieve and focus on this year, in Jesus name.

O Lord, here are some things I am thinking about. I ask You today to make known unto me the depths of these ideas and plans before me right now.....

(read out specific things or areas you need His clarification and direction)

In Jesus name

Father, remove from me any buried grudges or half-acknowledged enmity against anyone and every other thing that is blocking my spiritual vision and sensitivity.

Let every idol of personal opinions and conceptions, consciously and unconsciously, present in my heart, be melted away by the fire of the Holy Spirit, in Jesus name.

O Lord, give me the spirit of revelation and wisdom in the knowledge of You. Inspire and teach me what to do daily from now onwards, in Jesus name.

Henceforth, I destroy every spiritual blindness in my life. I curse the spirit of haste and impatience. I decree and declare that I will not fall under the manipulation of the spirits of confusion anymore, in the name of Jesus Christ.

O Lord, make Your way plain before me from now onwards and lead me in the path to take henceforth.

Teach me to know that which is worth knowing.

To love that which is worth loving,

And to dislike and disconnect from that which I must dislike and disconnect from.

Through the Holy Spirit, Lord, open my eyes and help me make the right decisions this year.

Guide and direct me in knowing Your mind and thoughts, for You are the One who reveals all secret things. Make known unto me Your choices for me in all issues, goals, ideas, and plans that I will embark on this year, in Jesus name of Jesus.

Today, in the name of Jesus Christ, I bind the activities of ....

- Lust and ungodly infatuation
- Family pressure
- Demonic manipulation in dreams
- Negative soul ties
- Attachments to wrong connections
- Confusing revelations and dreams
- Ungodly and unprofitable suggestions

- Haste and impatience.

I decree that I will not miss the mark this year, in Jesus name.

REMEMBER THIS…

"Hearing God's voice is the basis for experiencing His blessings in the famine."

DAY 10

PRESERVED BY HIS GRACE

Genesis 26: 7 - And the men of the place asked him about his wife, and he said, 'She is my sister;' for he was afraid to say, 'She is my wife' [thinking], lest the men of the place should kill me for Rebekah, because she is attractive and is beautiful to look upon (AMPC)

One beautiful thing about Scripture is that it is not telling us stories of perfect people. It tells us the good, the bad, and the ugly. And more importantly, it shows us that God didn't choose only perfect people for His purpose, nor is it only the perfect that He blesses. He chooses us the way we are and helps us become what He wants us to be.

Here is Isaac, a man who heard the voice of God a few weeks ago, a covenant son, filled with the knowledge of God's working with his father, yet he became afraid and told some awkward lies. How could he? What happened? Where was his fear of God?

Well, today, we need to learn that, sometimes, being caught up with our weakness is not a sign of a lack of fear of God. God's working in us and with us is not because we are perfect.

Yes, we will continue to trust, obey, and serve to the best of our ability. But we must never fall into the sin of thinking highly of our works as the reason God is using or blessing us.

> **Ephesians 2:8** - For by grace you have been saved through faith, and that not of yourselves; it is the gift of God

While God's grace is not a license to live and rejoice in sin, it is an assurance that God's got our backs no matter what happens. He's got our backs even when we're caught up in flaws and weaknesses.

DON'T CONDEMN YOURSELF; JUST REPENT

Have you made mistakes in the past? Have you missed your way in God? Are there some past decisions and actions that you now regret? Are you wondering if God can still use and bless you? Do you think that maybe the problems in your life are because of what you've done?

Today, hear the word of God: "Don't condemn yourself. It's not about your works. It's about His grace. God has not given up on you. He is still with you; He will always be with you."

Yes, repent from your sins and trust God to follow the ordained path for you. But stop condemning yourself because of your past mistakes and weaknesses. With God, there is a sure, new, and better beginning. The scripture says:

14 Let us, then, hold firmly to the faith we profess. For we have a great High Priest who has gone into the very presence of God—Jesus, the Son of God. 15 Our High Priest is not one who cannot feel sympathy for our weaknesses. On the contrary, we have a High Priest who was tempted in every way that we are, but did not sin.

16 Let us have confidence, then, and approach God's throne, where there is grace. There we will receive mercy and find grace to help us just when we need it. – Hebrews 4: 14-16

Through Christ, there is a great grace to start anew, become better, do better, and excel, no matter the issues the enemy comes up with

PRAYERS/DECLARATIONS

Heavenly Father,

Thank you that You do not count my errors, weaknesses, and failures. Thank You that Christ is sympathetic to my struggles and pains. Thank You for restoring my faith and confidence and reminding me that it is by grace we are saved through faith and not by works.

I pray, Father, this year, help me to never dwell on my past failures, weaknesses, and mistakes anymore. Help me only focus on Your love, wisdom, and the new things You are doing in my life and destiny, in Jesus name.

Today, I speak to myself and command myself to be confident in the Lord all through this year. I declare that I will be bold and step out and walk in the purpose of God for my life, and I will excel in all areas of life.

I am an all-inclusive victor. I prevail in all circumstances. I reject all forms of victim and loser mentality.

I will be a positive influence in my community this year. Wherever I go, and in whatever I do, I will excel and be a model for the Lord.

By the Holy Spirit, I will be profitable in my career, business, family, and in my work.

This year, I cast out from my life the spirits of laziness, procrastination, lack of commitment, worry, fear, and complaining.

O Lord, baptize me with grace and wisdom that will make me a positive influence in the lives of others. Use me to make people's lives better.

May whatever the enemy planted in my life and family, in the past, as a result of my spiritual laziness and sleepiness be uprooted and destroyed this day, in Jesus name.

Today, I cast out of my life anything that makes me powerless in the spirit world. Every door that I have opened out of ignorance, fear, or doubt that has enabled the devil to harass my life and family before now, I close them today and forever, in Jesus name.

From today and all through this year, I humble myself before the Lord. And I resist the devil and his demons. I resist fear, self-condemnation, self-guilt, and self-pity. I will be bold, smart, confident, and stand for what is right, in Jesus name.

This year, my light must shine. And through my light, others will also see the light. Through my light, the works of darkness will be defeated in others' lives, in the name of Jesus Christ.

This year, I will be an example of the abundant life and wisdom of God. I will distribute grace, wisdom, peace, and love to others in abundance. I will be an instrument of encouragement. And as I sow encouragement to others, I will reap help, support, and encouragement in every area of my life, in Jesus name

Today, I decree that the Lord is with me. He is my helper, my strength in weakness, and the lifter of my head. I shall not fear what man can do. I shall not fear mere mortals' plans, threats, and intentions, in Jesus name.

Amen.

REMEMBER THIS

We must never fall into the sin of thinking highly of our works as the reason God is using or blessing us.

DAY 11

STAY IN FAITH; GOD WILL SURELY INTERVENE IN YOUR HOME

Genesis 26:8-9 - When Isaac had been there a long time, Abimelek, king of the Philistines, looked down from a window and saw Isaac caressing his wife, Rebekah. So Abimelek summoned Isaac and said, "She is really your wife! Why did you say, 'She is my sister'?"

This is very interesting. I know we should be talking about how Isaac survived during the famine, how he planted and reaped a hundredfold return in the same year, and how he went on to become very wealthy even in the year of famine. That's what we are talking about, but it's important to capture all the various aspects of the story so that we can prepare our hearts for the miracles and blessings God has for our lives this year.

Notice in the verses today that Isaac and his wife, Rebekah, were on some kind of outing. They were enjoying themselves when the king noticed that Rebekah was Isaac's wife and not his sister, as he had earlier told them.

Okay, we talked about the lies part yesterday; let's talk about the other part today.

Isaac and his wife were in a strong harmony of spirit, soul, and body. This is evidenced in their romance. The Bible used the words "caressing his wife" to show the depth of love that the couple had.

The lesson today is that a united, supportive, and harmonious home front empowers a victorious and blessed life.

One thing I teach in the church is that you need to have a stable home to have a blessed life. I know it's not a popular teaching, but there is a level of glory that will never come to play in your life in a troubled home environment. The bible says:

> **1 Peter 3: 7** - In the same way, you husbands must give honor to your wives. Treat your wife with understanding as you live together. She may be weaker than you are, but she is your equal partner in God's gift of new life. Treat her as you should so your prayers will not be hindered.

We must seek a peaceful home and not just a successful life. I know this is dependent on several factors, but it must be our desire, too. It must be something we tell God every year. We must do our part and trust God to help us in areas we cannot help ourselves.

In my upcoming book, *21 Days Prayers for Your Family,* I teach that we are placed in our families by divine will. We are not in our families by accident. God allowed us to become members of our present families for a reason. And one of those reasons is to shine His light. We are there to be the reason God changes the stories of our families.

> "See, I have this day set thee over the nations and the kingdoms, to root out, and to pull down, and to destroy, and to throw down, to build, and to plant"
> – Jeremiah 1:10

You are a priest, a king, and a prophet over your family. As a priest, you're called to offer sacrifices on behalf of your family members. As a king, you're there to enforce divine order, and as a prophet, you're there to uproot what must be uprooted and plant and nurture what must be planted and nurtured.

There are four keys to taking back your family that I teach every year. These are powerful principles you should always apply.

KEY #1: YOU ARE GOD'S WATCHMAN

The moment you became a child of God through repentance, you became a priest, a king, and a prophet. These three special offices make you a spiritual watchman over your home.

You are not just a wife, husband, son, or daughter in your present family. You occupy spiritual positions that empowers you to enforce the will of God in that home. As long as you continue to offer sacrifices (intercession) for your home and continue to pray and decree, your family will be saved. They will be delivered from the works of darkness.

A watchman's primary responsibility is to thwart illegal activity at his employer's property. A watchman is also charged with protecting the interest of His employer, customers, clients, or residents from harm.

As God's watchman over your family, your presence forbids any illegal intrusion. You are called to represent God and tell the devil, *"I'm here. There's no space for you in this home."*

KEY #2: DON'T ACCEPT WHAT GOD FORBIDS

God put you in charge of your family to enforce His plan. You keep the devil where he belongs. You have the power and authority to do so.

> Thou shalt also decree a thing, and it shall be established unto thee: and the light shall shine upon thy ways - Job 22:28

You can influence your family's experiences through constant decrees, declarations, praise, and spiritual warfare.

Don't fight your battles physically. Don't try to quarrel your way out. Stay spiritually alert and keep on decreeing and declaring.

"But I've been praying," you say, "and nothing much has changed in my home."

Well, keep on doing that. Continue to intercede, decree, declare, bind, and loose. The changes are happening, and they will be made manifest because God is committed to honoring your prayers.

KEY #3: KEEP FAITH ALIVE

Someone said, "Your faith can move mountains, but your doubt can create them."

Faith does not make things easy, but it makes them possible.

Luke 18:1-8 tells the story of a widow who never gave up pressing for justice until the unbelieving judge decided to help her. Every day, she would go to the judge and say, *"Sir, you have to decide this matter for me. You have to represent me. I don't have money, but you need to help me."*

She kept pressing and pressing until the judge said, *"I have to do something about this woman. Though I'm not afraid of God or men, but because of this woman's persistence, I have to look into her case."*

Jesus then said, *"You see, imagine what this wicked judge said? Will not our just God defend and avenge His elect [His chosen ones] who cry out to Him day and night? Will He delay in providing justice on their behalf?"*

In other words, if a wicked man can be good when pressed repeatedly, how much more God, who is a good Father?

> ***God will honor your persistent prayers for your family. You must keep faith alive.***

When God got you saved, He didn't just have you in mind. He had your whole family in mind. So don't worry about your troublesome, unsaved family members. Don't let the devil keep you in worry and fear because of them. God knows how to reach out to them. And even at the very end, He will reach out to them. All you need to do is keep your faith alive. Your expectations and prayers will be answered.

KEY #4. IMAGINE THE CHANGE

Every time God is planning something big, He needs our cooperation. He said to Abraham in Genesis 13:15, *"I am giving all this land, as far as you can see..."*

God is limited only to the depth and height of our sight. If we don't accept and see in advance what God is saying, we limit the manifestation of His blessings and promises in our lives.

Today, God is speaking about your home, family, and children. He says, "What do you see?"

God says that your children will come to you from afar. They will be restored from prodigality. They will not be scattered. They will become the prayers you have prayed for them. Begin to see your children in the light of God's Word, not in the light of their present behaviors.

See your spouse and your marriage in the light of God's word. They may not be what you pray right now, but don't worry; your responsibility is to love, correct, support, and intercede. God is building them to Himself.

Today, pray for your home. Declare God's word over your family members. Tell the devil, *"This home is not for sale. We are not moved by what we see today. We are confident in God's word for our children and everyone in our bloodline."*

Claim victory for your family against sickness, prodigality, poverty, and rebellion, in Jesus name. Declare: *"God has made me a priest, a king, and a prophet in my home. Through my prayers, praises, and spiritual seeds, my family's destiny will be restored and rearranged in Jesus name."*

PRAYERS/DECLARATIONS

For Your Family

O Lord, my Father, I thank You today for Your Word about my family and my children. Thank You that You are at work in my family and in the lives of my children.

Today, Lord, I begin to see my home in the light of Your Word and not in the light of anyone's behaviors. I see my spouse saved, humble, and serving You.

I see my children saved, blessed, and serving You.

I see my home, my family, and every one of us reflecting Your glory forever and ever, in Jesus name.

Heavenly Father, You said it shall be unto me according to my faith. So I decree that my family is a center for peace, love, and excellence.

I decree that the love of God oozes out of my home from this day forward, like never before. I decree that my family is a blessing to this generation, in Jesus name.

O Lord, make me Your ambassador in my home - always believing and trusting You, always setting an example of peace, love, and support for everyone, in Jesus name.

Father, may Your Spirit take charge of my family members (name them) henceforth. Turn our hearts to each other and to Your Love and grace.

Help each member of my family be humble and gentle in our communications and be patient, bearing with one another's mistakes in love – even when we're tired, frustrated, angry, or hurt.

Please help us, Father, to make every effort to remain united in the Spirit in this home, in Jesus name.

O Lord Jesus Christ, I dedicate my family and home to You throughout this year. Rule and reign in our house. Be our Lord and Savior, in Jesus name.

For Your Marriage

Heavenly Father, I recognize that You are the One who instituted marriage to further Your will here on earth. Thank You for my partner, whom You have given to me.

Lord Jesus, I ask You to forgive me in every way I have tried to work out my relationship without You. How often do I think it is in my hand to make the best out of my partner.

Lord, forgive my ignorance and negative thinking.

You said in 2 Chronicles 7:14 that if I humble myself and confess my faults, that You will forgive me and heal my land.

Lord, in this case, my land is my relationship.

I confess my faults in thoughts, words, and actions in my relationship with my spouse and partner. Forgive me, cleanse me and let your mercy be made manifest in my marriage by the Blood of Jesus Christ.

Lord, I claim Your Forgiveness today. I claim Your grace and mercy to find help in my relationship, in Jesus name.

O Lord, I bring my partner before You today. I raise my relationship and marriage before Thee. O Lord, teach us to love You and to love and respect one another.

Help us to delight in You always. Help us to believe You at all times and trust Your work in our lives.

Draw us closer to You each day of our lives, Lord, both now and forever, in Jesus name.

Father, You said that as I delight myself in You, that You will give me the desires of my heart. That as I trust You, You will make my righteousness shine like the dawn.

Lord, I desire that You will prevail in my marriage and amplify Your love and understanding between me and my spouse, far greater than it used to be.

Cause us to continue to find favor with each other continually. Take away strife between us and bind us once again in Your love, in Jesus name.

I speak right now to the spirits of anger, conflict, hate, alcohol, addiction, and indecency; I bind you demons and command you all to pack your belongings and leave my life and that of my partner right now.

I command all demons causing strife, anger, quarreling, misunderstanding, thoughts of indecency, addiction to negativity, and separation to go into the abyss and remain there bound forever and ever, in Jesus name.

I decree today that my partner and I are humble and serving the LORD.

I decree that our hearts are arrested and bonded together in the spirit and in the physical.

This year, I pronounce increased peace, love, romance, understanding, respect, and cooperation between my spouse and me, in Jesus name.

Amen.

REMEMBER THIS…

As God's watchman over your household, your presence forbids any illegal intrusion in your family. You are called to represent God and tell the devil, "I'm here. There's no space for you in this home."

DAY 12

THE KING'S ORDER

Genesis 26:11 - So Abimelech charged all his people, saying, "He who touches this man or his wife shall surely be put to death."

Abimelech, a physical king, ordered that no one should touch Isaac or his family. The king's order said that anyone who touched him would die. Though he later fell out with Isaac due to Isaac's overwhelming success, but for a season, that order stayed active and provided a footing for Isaac's success and conquering of the land.

If a king's order can stand and work in favor of someone, how much more is the order of God, the King of kings. Today, remind yourself that there is a proclamation over your life. The King's order over you this year says

- "Touch not my anointed (you) and do my prophet (you) no harm."

- "No weapon formed against you shall prosper, And every tongue which rises against you in judgment you shall condemn."

This order is from the King of kings and the Lord of lords. The Almighty God Himself has decreed and declared that you will be safe and protected in the land, no matter what happens. You will prevail.

Stand on what God says and declare His protection over your life and family. His Words will never fall to the ground.

You will live and not die. No member of your family will die. It shall be well with you. God has spoken. He is the King of kings; His Words cannot change, neither will He change His mind like a physical king.

"For behold, the darkness shall cover the earth, and deep darkness the people; but the Lord will arise over you, and His glory will be seen upon you" – Isaiah 60:2

Darkness symbolizes evil, fear, diseases, loss, death, terrorism, confusion, and pain. God says that even though darkness prevails in the world, He will be your light.

The Psalmist confirms this in Psalm 91:

You shall not be afraid of the terror by night, nor of the arrow that flies by day, Nor of the pestilence that walks in darkness, nor of the destruction that lays waste at noonday.

A thousand may fall at your side, and ten thousand at your right hand, but it shall not come near you. Only with your eyes shall you look and see the reward of the wicked (Vs. 5-8).

God is saying that He will protect you, preserve you, and provide for you this year. You can trust Him and declare His protection.

PRAYERS/DECLARATIONS

Against the Powers Of Darkness

Heavenly Father,

I thank You for the victory that I have over the powers of satan through the death and resurrection of Jesus Christ.

Thank You for delivering us from the power of darkness and translating us into the kingdom of Your Son, Jesus Christ, in whom we have redemption because of His sacrifice, resulting in the forgiveness of our sins and the cancellation of the penalty of our sins (Colossians 1:13-15).

O Lord, I pray this day, any man or woman posing as a friend in my life and family, but is secretly working for my downfall, Father expose their intentions and frustrate their activities this year, in Jesus name.

May every agent of darkness assigned against my life this year become frustrated and bundled back into the abyss, in Jesus name.

Father, give me the wisdom to recognize when I am walking towards the traps of men and to be able to resist these traps.

I decree that by the Blood of Jesus Christ, myself, my family, my children, and my lineage, henceforth, belong to the covenant of salvation in Christ. We are no longer victims of evil blood covenants, in Jesus name.

Father, in every area of my life, I claim the assistance, support, and help of Your angels assigned to protect and guide me this year. I release Your angels to go right now, and all through this year, and correct every negative information that the enemy has spread about me, in Jesus name.

I decree and declare that I and every member of my family shall be protected and preserved from all troubles this year ..., in the name of Jesus Christ.

Psalm 91

(Prayerphrased)

I declare according to Psalm 91 ...

All through this year, I and my family will dwell in the secret place of the Almighty God. We shall remain established under His shadow where no enemy can withstand His power.

2 We will say of the Lord, He is our Refuge and our Fortress; our God, whom we depend on, whom we put our trust.

3Every day in this year, God will deliver us from every trap of the enemy and from all deadly diseases that attack the world

4 He will shield us with His feathers, and under His arms shall we find refuge, for He is faithful always. He is our armor and our shield.

5Today, I declare that we shall not be afraid of the terrors of the night, nor of the arrows and evil plots and slanders that happens during the day.

6We shall not fear the pestilence (diseases) that threatens in darkness, nor of the destructions and sudden deaths that looms and lays waste at noonday.

7Even if a thousand falls at our side and ten thousand at our right hand, no evil shall come near us. 8 We will only be a spectator over the attacks and punishments of the wicked.

---

9 The Lord is our refuge, and the Almighty God is our dwelling place... so 10there shall no evil befall us, nor any infection or calamity come near our dwelling.

11For God's angels are under instruction to cover us, to escort, to defend and preserve us in all our ways. 12They shall bear us up on their hands, and we will never dash our foot against a stone.

13All through this year, if we encounter or step on lions and snakes, witches and wizards, or evil people, we will crush them under our foot because God is with us

14 He will deliver us continually from the intentions of the wicked; He will set us on high, because of His name; His mercy, love, and kindness will never forsake us, forever and ever.

15This year, God will answer our prayers when we call on Him. He will be with us at all times as He promised. In troubles, He will be with us;

He will deliver us and bring us to a place of honor, and ₁₆with long life will He satisfy us and show us His salvation, in Jesus name.

Amen.

REMEMBER THIS…

"Even if the powers of darkness are stirred against the world in the form of pestilence, hunger, insecurity, and other attacks, we will be spared."

DAY 13

A HUNDREDFOLD GRACE

Genesis 26: 12-13 — ₁₂Then Isaac sowed in that land, and reaped in the same year a hundredfold; and the Lord blessed him. ₁₃The man began to prosper, and continued prospering until he became very prosperous; ₁₄for he had possessions of flocks and possessions of herds and a great number of servants. So the Philistines envied him.

Some weeks ago, I asked our over 60,000 Facebook audience a question and said, *"If you knew that harvest was guaranteed, what would you plant?"*

I received over 190 responses, with most comments saying something like, "I will plant love, joy, peace, happiness.... I will plant the seed of salvation, wisdom, restoration, unity, open doors, divine breakthrough, divine connections, financial breakthrough, marital settlement, good health, long life, safety, all-around blessings, etc."

As spiritual and powerful as these responses sounded, that wasn't what I had in mind when I asked that question. What I meant to ask was,

- If you were sure nothing could stop you, what would you do in the new year?

- If you were sure that you would succeed, what business would you start, or what changes would you make to move your life forward?

Today, God is saying to you, "*I am with you and will always be with you. Your year and your future are guaranteed. Don't be afraid to sow your seeds and take steps of faith that align with your expectations. There is a hundredfold grace released over your life. Your seeds and actions of faith will not fail. The same mystery at work in the life of Isaac is at work in your life."*

₅ Your eyes will shine with joy, your hearts will thrill, for merchants from around the world will flow to you, bringing you the wealth of many lands. ₆ Vast droves of camels will converge upon you, dromedaries from Midian and Sheba and Ephah too, bringing gold and incense to add to the praise of God. ₇ The flocks of Kedar shall be given you, and the rams of Nabaioth for my altars, and I will glorify my glorious Temple in that day – Isaiah 60: 5-7

What do you see in this scripture?

Okay, close your eyes for a moment and imagine merchants (traders, businessmen, and women) from around the world coming to you, bringing you the wealth of many lands. Imagine vast droves of cars converging around you, emissaries from different countries, bringing gold and incense to add to the praise of God in your life.

> ***Expect tremendous supernatural intervention in your finances this year, in Jesus name.***

There is a hundredfold grace released in your life. Look beyond your immediate needs and expand your vision.

Allow the Holy Spirit to breathe into you new ideas and dreams. Stop focusing on how to survive or get by. Receive bigger pictures of new goals in your heart, and receive boldness to step out in faith, sow your seeds, and receive hundredfold returns.

UNLOCKING A HUNDREDFOLD GRACE

To unlock a hundredfold grace this year, you must be spiritually alert. Why? Because God answers our breakthrough prayers by dropping ideas or supernatural thoughts in our spirits. These may be new ideas on approaching your current endeavor, where to drop your CV, some persons to approach for a business discussion, or new business to venture into. When these unplanned thoughts drop in your spirit, don't despise them. Recognize them and follow their recommendations.

In Luke chapter 5, Peter toiled all night without catching a single fish. He and his colleagues were frustrated and needed a breakthrough. Jesus came on board and, after using his boat, told him to cast his net again into the water.

Peter tried to explain to Jesus that fishes don't show up at such times, that it makes no sense trying to catch fishes during the day, from the same water where they couldn't find a single fish when the waters were quiet. Nevertheless, he decided to prove his theory to Christ by casting his net into the water. The Bible says:

> 6 When they had done so, they caught such a large number of fish that their nets began to break. 7 So they signaled their partners in the other boat to

come and help them, and they came and filled both boats so full that they began to sink.

Jesus was like, *"Hey, Peter! I know you've failed in this business. But go ahead and try again. This time, you have my Word. A hundredfold grace is on your life."*

Peter tried again, and boom, his nets were filled with fishes, so much that he needed help to draw them out of the same water he had failed initially

One thing about the instructions or inspired ideas God puts in our hearts from our prayers and fasting is that they contain the answers we seek. That is why it is essential to recognize these divine thoughts, write them down, and follow them.

This year, sow your seeds and give your offerings in confidence. But go beyond that. Spend much time praying in the Holy Spirit and discern what God is saying in your heart and follow them. They may not look easy. They may require a lot of courage. But that's how to activate the hundredfold grace in your life.

> *Don't look for direction and answers to your prayers outside. They are in the deepest parts of your belly. You only need to draw them out through praying in the Holy Ghost and intense quietness.*

Be spiritually alert and sensitive to the steps God wants you to take and the changes He wants you to make, and follow them. As shared earlier, His direction is the key to activating His hundredfold grace.

PRAYERS/DECLARATIONS

Heavenly Father, thank You for it is Your will that I prosper and be in good health.

Thank You because I am confident that this year is a year of abundance of wealth for me and my household.

I give You praise because You delight in the prosperity of Your people.

I give You praise because all through this year, You will supply our needs according to Your riches in Christ Jesus.

Receive my praise today in Jesus name.

O Lord, how often do I think that prosperity, money, and success are by my efforts and decisions.

Lord, I come to You this day and confess my ignorance and pride. Forgive me for not giving

You the ultimate place in my finances in the past. Forgive me, Lord. Let Your mercy prevail over me this day, in Jesus name.

O Lord, by the Blood of Jesus Christ, I receive forgiveness from any form of greed and financial impropriety in the past.

Lord Jesus, throughout this year and beyond, let Your Blood speak for me financially, in Jesus name.

---

*It is written in **Job 36:11** that if I obey and serve God, I will spend my days in prosperity and my years in plenty.*

Lord, I desire to serve and obey You from this. I come to You right now and ask for the grace to be a doer of the Word on finances and in every aspect of life, in Jesus name.

Father, I surrender my desires to You. Work in me to desire and pursue only things that align with Your plans for my life.

Help me to only choose investments, businesses, careers, and jobs that align with Your grand purpose for my life.

Deliver me from my own plans, which may seem reasonable in my eyes but are the ways of death.

Cause me to recognize Your peace, which is a signal of progress, or Your internal struggle, which is a sign of retreat, in Jesus name.

Lord, forgive and restore whatever the enemy has tinkered with in my life, family, and destiny due to not listening to Your instructions and not following your guidance in the past, in Jesus name.

Today, I pray for restoration in my spirit, soul, body, health, and finances.

Lord, remove any persistent grudge buried in my heart against anyone; free me from unforgiveness, hostility, and every other thing blocking my vision and hearing, in the name of Jesus Christ.

Through the Holy Spirit, Father, remind me what You said to me in the past that I ignored or unknowingly walked away from. Teach me how to receive answers to my financial breakthrough prayers and desires henceforth.

Show me how to make profit, how to live debt-free, and how to create wealth, in Jesus name.

I declare that, in the name of Jesus Christ...

A hundredfold grace is at work in my life.

I am walking into my green pastures.

All my efforts will yield hundredfold returns this year.

Because God cares for me and wants it to be well with me, I reject every attack of the devil over my finances, in Jesus name.

I untie my finances from the hold of the devil and decree supernatural financial supplies in my possession from this day forward, in the name of Jesus Christ.

May whatever the devil has done in my mind and in my life, causing me to be spiritually blind and unable to access ideas and revelations from God about my finances, be destroyed, in Jesus name.

I declare that...

God is ordering my steps; He is showing me what to do regarding my finances; I am getting connected to everyone connected to my breakthrough.

I am receiving the right jobs, the right offers, the right business open doors, the right investments and savings plans, and the right money-making opportunities, in the name of Jesus Christ.

I pray today, Lord ...When I lay down to sleep, may my dreams bring me clarity about Your direction;

When I am discussing with people, may my discussions bring me clarity;

When I am are thinking of what to do, may my thoughts bring me clarity;

May there be no more confusion in my mind, in the name of Jesus Christ.

Father, thank You for directing and guiding me over my finances this year. Thank You for a hundredfold grace at work in my life. Just like Isaac, I know what to do, where to stay, what to plant, and how to grow, in Jesus name, I pray.

Amen.

REMEMBER THIS

"There is a hundredfold grace released in your life. Look beyond your immediate needs and expand your vision."

DAY 14

YOU'VE GOT SOMETHING TO DO

Genesis 26: 12-13 — ₁₂Then Isaac sowed in that land, and reaped in the same year a hundredfold; and the Lord blessed him. ₁₃The man began to prosper, and continued prospering until he became very prosperous; ₁₄for he had possessions of flocks and possessions of herds and a great number of servants. So the Philistines envied him.

Notice here that even though Isaac was a covenant son and walked in obedience, he still didn't prosper without work. He planted crops in a year of drought. There was no physical motivation or signs to grow crops that year, but he did. He had genuine reasons to stay off work and observe like others, but he chose to farm. Why? I guess he must have read from the

Spirit the Wisdom of Solomon in Ecclesiastes 11: 4,6, which says:

> ₄ Farmers who wait for perfect weather never plant. If they watch every cloud, they never harvest.... ₆ Plant your seed in the morning and keep busy all afternoon, for you don't know if profit will come from one activity or another — or maybe both (NLT).

There will never be a perfect time to plant your seeds; that is, an ideal time to start or do something God is laying in your heart to do.

> *Sometimes, the weather will not be favorable, and there may not be physical signs that God is leading you.*

But once you have prayed about it over and over and the assurance is right there in your spirit, then you must plant your seeds in the morning and keep busy all afternoon. You must look away from the unfavorable circumstances and focus on the Word of God and who we are in Him.

There is always something to do to command the miracles we pray for in our lives. And I pray that your heart will discern what you must do right now about the situation in your life.

It was not easy for Isaac to sow seeds in a year of drought and national crisis. He would have just relaxed and watched like others if he had considered the obstacles. Sowing that year required a lot of physical and mental effort. He had to find a way to get water to water his crops. He had to dig wells.

I asked myself some time ago, "If God spoke to Isaac, why did he need to work that hard still? I thought because God spoke to him, things would have just moved on without any obstacle. Why didn't it rain on his side of the country and farm? Why didn't he sit in his house while God sends blessings and supplies after him?"

Well, it turns out that's not how God ordained things to run. And sometimes, we can misread God in this area.

Just because God said we should stay in a place, do something, or start a project, does not mean that things would be easy. It does not mean that we would not need to work so hard.

> *Don't expect everything to be easy because you fasted and prayed or because you're sure God inspired you to take the steps you're currently taking. Things may not be easy initially, but your eventual victory is guaranteed. You'll prevail, no matter what happens.*

So, embrace the work aspect of the divine plan, even while depending on God's word to come to pass. A hundredfold grace is activated when we do our part. God's grace also works with work

THINK FORWARD

I heard Bishop David Oyedepo once say that "What you have is enough if you can think enough." I didn't believe him immediately because I was in the middle of something and was praying and believing that I needed more things to get some things done. But after some critical mental imagination, I felt, *"Maybe I can do something meaningful with what I already have."*

We are in a world where it's not always enough. Everyone is looking for more. And the truth is that we do need more. But we fail to ask ourselves if we have used all we truly have.

We constantly see obstacles and complain about the problems we can't handle and what we don't have. But have we truly employed all of God's resources with us?

Isaac could have complained of the famine, and you know what, he'd be right not to plant anything that year. But while everyone was complaining about the problems, he was thinking of the way forward. Consequently, God gave him the wisdom of digging wells. It didn't work the first and second time, but he continued until he broke through.

The Holy Spirit is giving me these words for you right now:

> "You can go forward from where you are right now. You can grow and advance. Everything you need is already provided. Stop focusing on your limitations. Focus on the ability of God and the way forward. You are unstoppable."

If you are ever pressured to think at all, then only think forward. Think about how to go forward and not on the problems stopping you.

Do you need to take some classes in computer or something else?

Well, if that's a way to move forward in some way this year, then embrace it. Enroll in a class today.

Do you need to close a relationship door and trust God for a new beginning?

If that's one way forward in your life right now, then embrace it. Stop wasting time trying to wake up a dead horse, trying to make a dead engine move.

Do you need to create a new product or modify an existing product line?

Again, if that's one way forward in your life right now, then get started. Gather the details and start making the calls.

We can't keep doing things in old ways without improving ourselves and our systems and only depend on prayer and fasting for a breakthrough. There is a time to pray, and there is a time to work forward.

Isaac was a covenant son led by God. Yet he faced obstacles until he improvised his way forward by digging wells. God didn't drill the wells for him. He dug them. He innovated his way forward.

Isaac provided a solution leveraging the technology of his time. While others continued to wait for rain, he improvised an alternative and used the same to grow his farm. So why wouldn't he prosper? Why wouldn't he, the same year, become so rich that his host country envied him?

Today, I challenge you to surrender to the Holy Spirit and let Him inspire your heart on ways to go forward this year. Instead of praying and waiting for handouts, windfalls, and quick help to fix your urgent problems, pray for God's empowerment that makes you come up with definite steps forward in your life.

Waiting on God is excellent, but waiting for God is risky. While the first is praying, fasting, reading scriptures, and listening for His direction and inspiration, the second is waiting for Him to come and do things for us instead of using His ability to do the things He is inspiring us to do. Wait on God, but don't wait for Him.

Receive grace that challenges you to know that there is always a way forward, no matter where you are now, in Jesus name.

PRAYERS/DECLARATIONS

Heavenly Father,

Empower me to think forward this year. By Your Spirit, show me things I must do to make progress and see the changes and miracles I desire in my life.

As Isaac did not let the drought stop him, I declare that I will not allow the world's situation to affect whatever I will do this year.

I am empowered by God to succeed morning, afternoon, and night. My labor will be fruitful.

By the wisdom of God, I will never be stranded at any point in my life again. I will know what to do at all times to move forward in my spiritual, relational, career, business, and financial life, in Jesus name.

Amen.

REMEMBER THIS

"Surrender to the Holy Spirit and let Him inspire your heart on ways to go forward."

DAY 15

ENEMIES CANNOT STOP YOU

Genesis 26: 15-22 ₁₅ Now the Philistines had stopped up all the wells which his father's servants had dug in the days of Abraham his father, and they had filled them with earth. ₁₆ And Abimelech said to Isaac, "Go away from us, for you are much mightier than we."

₁₇ Then Isaac departed from there and pitched his tent in the Valley of Gerar, and dwelt there. ₁₈ And Isaac dug again the wells of water which they had dug in the days of Abraham his father, for the Philistines had stopped them up after the death of Abraham. He called them by the names which his father had called them.

₁₉ Also Isaac's servants dug in the valley, and found a well of running water there. ₂₀ But the herdsmen of Gerar quarreled with Isaac's herdsmen, saying, "The water is ours." So he called the name of the well Esek because they quarreled with him.

₂₁Then they dug another well, and they quarreled over that one also. So he called its name Sitnah. ₂₂ And he moved from there and dug another well, and they did not quarrel over it. So he called its name Rehoboth because he said, "For now the Lord has made room for us, and we shall be fruitful in the land."

Isaac faced many oppositions even in the same year that he planted and reaped a hundredfold. The entire nation envied him. The king reneged on his word and asked him to leave the country. The residents tried hard to cheat him. They fought to destroy his ancestral wealth and his efforts. Yet he went ahead to sow in the same year. What can we learn from all that?

First, God's blessings always attract opposition. The covenant that you're under its coverage will provoke demonic reactions and strange situations that you will not like. From time to time, you may have hostilities, conflicts, battles, and circumstances that can make you wonder what's happening. Nonetheless, know that you're sufficiently equipped to overcome whatever the enemy throws at you.

> ***Oppositions and hostile situations are not proof that God is not with you. God is with you even in your oppositions and challenges.***

No one wishes to have battles in their lives. No one likes to have oppositions and hostilities in their endeavors. Isaac did not wish to have his father's wells closed and his wells dubiously taken. These battles and oppositions just happen, sometimes, as a spiritual reaction to God's presence and blessings in our lives.

The battles in your life may not be because you committed some particular sins. It's just the way it is. The enemy is reacting against your unique placement in God's agenda.

But remember this: Your future is not in the hand of the opposition and enemies. Your future is in the hand of God. And God will never allow what you cannot overcome to come your way.

Don't focus on the size of the battle before you. Focus on the size of God with you. If God is for us, no one can succeed against us. They may try, but they will always fail. And we will always win.

There are four areas where the enemy attacked Isaac, and I want you to watch out for these areas. Stand against them and walk in the victory God has ordained for us.

We must not be ignorant of the devices of the devil. We must equip ourselves and reject every attack of satan this year.

ATTACK #1. ENVY AND JEALOUSY

₁₄ He owned flocks, herds, and a great supply of servants, **and the Philistines envied him**.

One of the biggest mysteries of life that has always baffled me is the knowledge that some people are not happy with the progress of others. They want someone never to grow or succeed. As long as you are unimportant and needy, they're okay. But the moment you start growing and becoming less needy, they raise eyebrows, to the extent of trying to hurt you.

I always find it hard to understand why the world is like that. I mean, people should be happy with the progress of others. After all, one man's progress does not stop another person's progress. So, why do some people hate to see others make progress?

Envy is an age-long demonic device that we will continue to deal with till the end of time. It was one of the forces unleashed by the enemy against Isaac in the year that he sowed and reaped a hundredfold. And God is calling our attention to watch out for the spirit of envy and stand guard against it.

The moment God's blessings began to show in the life of Isaac, the enemy stirred the minds of the people to start hating him. And this led them to do other things against him.

> *Do not think that everyone will like you or celebrate with you from their hearts. So, don't make it a goal to please every one. Please God and yourself. Focus on your dreams and not on how to make everyone happy.*

You will have those who smile with you openly but envy and wish you ruin secretly. Joseph's brothers envied his dreams of a future higher than theirs. They got consumed with the threat of his vision and sold him to an enemy. Although Joseph's vision did not stop them from having their own dreams, envy led them to try to ruin their brother's life.

Cain killed Abel because Abel's prayer was answered while his own was not. Instead of correcting his mistakes before God, he plotted and killed his brother so that he would not live to enjoy the benefits of that answered prayer.

An older prophet deceived a younger prophet and had him killed because he felt threatened by the ministry of the upcoming young man. He had to take him out of the way.

Envy and jealousy can cause people to go out of their way to destroy what they cannot build.

This year, watch out for the spirit of envy. Reject it in your own life and be spiritually alert about it from others. Celebrate with others when they are blessed and wish others well. And then be careful with people who will be possessed with the spirit of envy against you.

Be careful of those who feel you are succeeding too fast, who cannot understand why you are rising nonstop while they're not.

Be careful of those who think your family is in peace while theirs are not, who feel you already have children while they're not even married.

Watch out for people who think God is blessing you more than them or believe you are why their blessings are not forthcoming.

Sometimes people react to God's blessing in our lives by envy and jealousy. Even though we are not their problems, the devil can use them to cause havoc if we don't stay alert and in prayers against the operation of the spirit of envy.

I wish I could tell you that you will not have opposition this year. I wish I could tell you that it will be a smooth ride all through, without anything offending or trying to hurt you. I wish I could tell you that everyone will love you and pamper you. I want to, but I can't. If I do, that would be lying to you. I would be deceiving you with such a message.

What I know is that, like Isaac, you will come out stronger, no matter what happens. But prepare your mind to resist the devil and his devices, and they will flee.

ATTACK #2. WRECKING HIS CAPITAL

Genesis 26: 15 - Now the Philistines had stopped up all the wells which his father's servants had dug in the days of Abraham, his father, and they had filled them with earth.

This was another attack on Isaac. His father's wells were a tremendous leverage for him. Imagine if those wells were not stopped. They could have reduced his stress and made life easier for him. Unfortunately, the enemies tried to destroy this capital. Their goal was to frustrate him. They wanted him to be like them – crying, begging, and waiting for state intervention.

Thankfully, Isaac knew better. He knew that the covenant operating in his life was his major capital. You can stop the wells, but as long as you cannot stop the covenant and his faith, he was fine. He would always bounce back better. And that's what happened.

> [18] Isaac reopened the wells that had been dug in the time of his father Abraham, which the Philistines had stopped up after Abraham died, and he gave them the same names his father had given them (NIV).

You see that. If your faith says yes, God will not say no. The enemy may try, but they cannot stop you. The attacks and battles in your life right now cannot stop God's plans for your life.

Keep your faith alive because your faith is the most outstanding capital against the forces of darkness. As Isaac restored his father's wells despite the enemies' attacks, you will restore whatever has been stolen from your life, in Jesus name.

ATTACK #3. BUSY WITH IRRELEVANT ISSUES

₁₉Also, Isaac's servants dug in the valley and found a well of running water there. ₂₀But the herdsmen of Gerar quarreled with Isaac's herdsmen, saying, "The water is ours." So he called the name of the well Esek because they quarreled with him.

This was another attack on Isaac. The herdsmen of Gerar wanted to start a fight. But Isaac, again, by the Spirit, knew what to do. The quarrel was a trap to keep him busy with irrelevant issues. But he knew that if he could dig that well, he could also dig another one. So he wisely avoided the quarrel and focused on what mattered most.

King Solomon said:

"The beginning of strife is as when water first trickles from a crack in a dam; therefore stop contention before it becomes worse and quarreling breaks out" (Proverbs 17: 14 - AMPC).

Isaac seemed to see this advice even before it was written. He somehow knew that it was better to keep off from a quarrel before it fully broke out. Why? Because a quarrel or a fight is a distraction from the enemy designed to stop people from reaching their primary goals.

> *Sometimes the enemy creates quarreling situations and events to keep us busy with irrelevant issues.*

Most online arguments about tithing are examples of such issues the enemy wants us to continue arguing about while he goes about stealing, killing, and destroying.

This year, don't let the enemy keep you busy with things that do not have eternal significance or something that does not build up your faith. Resist any activity designed to trap you in quarrels, arguments, and strifes. Resist and reject them because the more you focus on fights and quarrels, the lesser you will realize God's plans for your life.

My pastor, Dr Dennis Inyang, said, "You need to know when to retreat and when to advance, when to speak and when to keep mute, when to stay and when to let go. Don't fight needless battles that jeopardize your life and future. Confrontation is not always a winning strategy!"

> *Know when to let an issue go, and trust God for a new beginning. Know when to ignore a quarrel to win the main battle.*

Of course, you don't have to let people take advantage of you unnecessarily, but you must learn to avoid chitty-chatty gossips, lies, criticisms, and hearsays. See beyond the quarrelsome things people are saying and doing. Avoid the distractions and focus on what matters.

Before every Rehoboth (expansion, growth, opportunity), beware of Esek (strife, quarrel, disagreement). And remember that if Isaac had continued to quarrel over Esek, he would not have gotten to Rehoboth.

ATTACK #4. BITTERNESS AND ENMITY

After trying so hard but failing to keep Isaac busy with quarreling, the opposition came up with something else. They graduated the quarrel into enmity.

> [21] Then his servants dug another well, and they quarreled over that also; so he named it Sitnah – enmity (AMPC).

The dictionary says enmity is a deep and bitter hatred, usually shared between enemies. It is a higher level of quarreling. At this level, it's no longer just an exchange of words; it's a bitter rivalry.

Isaac could have refused to give up this second well, and who knows, the rivalry may have continued until this day. It was enough that he let go of the first well for the sake of peace. He was just a migrant, but the second one, no, no, no. They were biting more than allowed.

However, Isaac avoided the enmity and moved on. He refused to welcome the grudges and bitterness. There was no place for enmity in his heart. Whatever would keep him in bitterness was not worth it.

To advance and reach our Rehoboth, we must watch out for bitterness. Watch out for things that will make you bitter, and don't let them succeed. Why? Because bitterness defiles and destroys.

The Bible says:

> **Hebrews 12:15** - See to it that no one fails to obtain the grace of God; that no "root of bitterness" springs up and causes trouble, and by it many become defiled;

Ephesians 4:26, 31-32 - Be angry and do not sin; do not let the sun go down on your anger ... Let all bitterness and wrath and anger and clamor and slander be put away from you, along with all malice. Be kind to one another, tenderhearted, forgiving one another, as God in Christ forgave you.

Tell the enemy to keep the grudges, enmity, and bitterness to himself this year. It's not for you. Like Isaac, you will not stay on the mountain of enmity and miss the realm of a hundredfold.

Receive grace and wisdom to let go of what needs to be let go this year. Receive grace to give no room to bitterness and enmity in your heart. Receive grace to walk away from arguments, quarrels, and situations that are designed to waste your time. Receive grace and wisdom to walk away from relationships that are satan's traps in your life. Receive grace to focus on self-growth, love, and worship from a pure heart, in Jesus name.

This year, I believe that no weapon formed against you shall prosper. You will prevail against the enemy because you are equipped and prepared. You are unstoppable.

PRAYERS/DECLARATIONS

In the name of Jesus Christ,

I declare that...I am unstoppable.

I will not be a victim of the forces of envy, bitterness, enmity, and dwelling on irrelevant issues.

My divinely released capital and resources will not be stopped or destroyed by demonic forces.

I cancel every attack targeted at my faith and boldness, in Jesus name

---

Nothing can stop me this year.

I receive grace and wisdom to navigate through any situation that is causing fear and worry in my life right now. I receive grace and knowledge to handle relationships, connections, and people's opinions that are standing against God's purpose in my life. And I receive grace to let go of what needs to be let go, in the name of Jesus Christ.

God is with me always

Nothing and no one can stand against me.

I am justified by His love, grace, faith, and the Blood of Jesus Christ. So, nothing and no one can accuse me or bring any charge against me

Nothing can separate me from the love of Christ.

In all things, in all situations, I am more than a conqueror through Christ. I overcome and win in everything, in Jesus name.

Amen.

REMEMBER THIS

Your future is not in the hand of the opposition and enemies. Your future is in the hand of God... Don't focus on the size of the battle before you. Focus on the size of God with you.

DAY 16

DON'T STOP DIGGING

And he moved from there and dug another well, and they did not quarrel over it. So he called its name Rehoboth because he said, "For now the Lord has made room for us, and we shall be fruitful in the land." - **Genesis 26: 22**

So Isaac dug two wells, but the citizens claimed ownership of them and chased him away. He and his staff labored so hard to dig those wells; remember, it was in a time of national drought; there was no rain, so this was a tough feat to achieve. Yet when they found water, the lazy residents, with their entitlement mentality, stopped them from profiting from their labors.

Let's imagine that it was some of us today. I know, it's not your portion. But just imagine that this happened to some of us today. The first and second time we tried and suffered such a setback was enough to say, "I think I need some deliverance. I don't think God is in this thing. I need to get out of this town. I heard wrongly."

But that was not Isaac. He moved on. He went elsewhere and continued digging until the enemies could no longer stop him.

I am convinced that Isaac had all kinds of emotions and questions. He must have asked himself several times, "What's happening? Where is the proof of God with us? What should we do next? Where should we go?"

He felt bad, but he did not give up. He questioned the proof of God with him, but he did not walk away in defeat. He even changed location but did not retire to his house in self-pity. He moved on.

You see, it's not wrong to ask questions or wonder what's happening. It's not wrong to query ourselves and have all the emotions we have after setbacks, failure, and disappointment.

> ***God does not condemn us for displaying our humanity when troubles and obstacles confront us. He's our Father and knows our weaknesses and sorrows. Our secret tears and questions are also prayers before Him.***

However, what is wrong is giving up and not trying again, stopping halfway and dwelling on our failures so much that we don't attempt to go forward one more time. That's what is wrong. That's what God does not want us to do.

Today, God is saying to you, "Don't stop digging for water. If you failed before, rise and try again. You may change location and change strategy. You may change course, change tools, and change workers. You may pray more, fast more, and attend more training. But don't stop digging. Don't stop trying. It is not more deliverance you need. You need more patience and persistence."

The third time that Isaac tried, he succeeded. He entered into his Rehoboth season and then said, "God has made room for us, and we shall be fruitful in the land."

But just imagine that he packed up and left without the third attempt. Just imagine that he said, "I've had enough. The challenges and battles are just too much. God is not helping us; we're not seeing any of His miracles."

If Isaac had abandoned the *well project* after the second attempt, he would not have found Rehoboth. If he had let his emotions take the better part of him, he might not have reaped a hundredfold return the same year, so much that he became the envy of a nation.

Beloved, don't let your gifts and talents die. Don't fold up and run away. Don't pack up. That's not the next thing to do. Find ways to try again, and again, and again. You will surely enter into your Rehoboth.

No matter where you are today, believe again. Try again. Don't stop just because things got bad. Focus on God and not on what the enemy has done. Focus on God and not on what could have happened that didn't happen.

Focus on God and not on what you feel. Your feelings will always change, but God will not. Like Isaac's case, everything about you will end in praise. God will never disappoint you.

PRAYERS/DECLARATIONS

Today, O Lord,

I command the doubts, fears, and anxieties in me to leave and never return.

I declare that God is concerned about me.

He loves me, He cares for me, and He will never let me down

I will not be put to shame or disappointed.

My joy will never be cut short.

In the name of Jesus Christ, I receive grace to keep on digging, to keep on believing, and to keep on moving forward.

I declare that there's no going back for me. God is at work in my life, and everything about me is getting better.

This is my year of Rehoboth.

God has made room for me, and I will be fruitful in the land. I will build and expand.

Whoever rises to fight against my progress will scatter in seven ways.

Every agent of darkness projected against my labor will die by fire.

I declare today, like Isaac, everything about me this year will end in praise.

My labor will be fruitful. My prayers will be answered. And I shall enjoy a hundredfold increase in every aspect of my life, in Jesus name.

Amen.

REMEMBER THIS

No matter where you are today, believe again. Don't stop just because things got bad. Focus on God and not on what the enemy has done.

SECTION 2

GENERAL

PRAYERS

The prayers in this section are repeated from past editions of the series, ***New Year Prayers***. They are usually prayer points that we pray no matter what the year's theme is. You will be blessed as you pray these prayers.

DAY 17

PRERS FOR OTHERS

Now all things are of God, who has reconciled us to Himself through Jesus Christ and has given us the ministry of reconciliation - **2 Cor. 5:18**

God has given every believer the ministry of reconciliation. We are God's partners in reuniting men back to Him. The job of bringing others to salvation is not only for pastors, prophets, and evangelists. It is for every Christian. We're saved to save others.

If you're confused about what God is calling you to do, start by accepting that you have received a ministry of reconciliation from Him. Then begin to look for avenues to share the love of Christ with your community of influence; start to invest in the salvation of others without making noise about it. As you stay faithful with what is already revealed, what is not revealed will be revealed.

There is always something we can do in our capacities to urge others to accept the salvation of the Lord Jesus Christ. Heartfelt prayer is one of them.

So today's prayer will be focused on praying for the salvation of others. Come to God in humility and sincerely pray for persons in your family, neighborhood, or community that need Jesus.

We're not going to pray some general prayers of, "Lord, save these people in this community." No. We will list the names of a few persons on paper and pray for their genuine salvation. Jesus said:

> I tell you that in the same way, there will be more rejoicing in heaven over one sinner who repents than over ninety-nine righteous persons who do not need to repent - Luke 15:7.

Let us create joy in heaven by genuinely praying for the salvation and healing of others. Why?

1. IT IS THE WILL OF GOD

As Christians, we are priests to our God. And one of the duties of a priest is to offer sacrifices on behalf of others.

> **2 Peter 2:5** - Like living stones, let yourselves be assembled into a spiritual house, a holy order of priests who offer up spiritual sacrifices that will be acceptable to God through Jesus the Anointed (THE VOICE).

We can offer sacrifices on behalf of others by praying for them.

2. SEEDS THAT WILL COME BACK

> Genesis 8:22 - While the earth remains, seedtime and harvest, cold and heat, winter and summer, and day and night shall not cease.

We will always need prayers at one point or the other. Maybe not now, but we will need genuine people to stand with us in prayer at some point in our lives. When those times come, the prayer seeds we have sown will multiply back to us.

3. IT EMPOWERS OUR PRAYERS

> When Job prayed for his friends, the Lord restored his fortunes. In fact, the Lord gave him twice as much as before! - Job 42:10 (NLT)

This is one of my favorite scriptures. Job was restored by praying for his friends. When we pray for others, our prayers are empowered for answers.

4. OUR HEARTS ARE MELTED

When we pray for others, we see the world from the lenses of others; we see others' hurts, and our hearts are melted with compassion.

Praying for others can make you more loving, forgiving, and tolerant. It will make you more humble and reverent because you will begin to discover that what you call a problem is small compared to what others are going through.

5. GOD IN THE LIVES OF OTHERS

When we pray for others, we recognize that God is the One in charge of those we pray for, and He lets us contribute to His work in their lives. It's a privilege.

6. WE ACTIVATE ETERNAL REWARDS

Jesus said in Matthew 25: 35-40:

35 For I was hungry, and you fed me. I was thirsty, and you gave me a drink. I was a stranger, and you invited me into your home. 36 I was naked, and you gave me clothing. I was sick, and you cared for me. I was in prison, and you visited me.'

37 "Then these righteous ones will reply, 'Lord, when did we ever see you hungry and feed you? Or thirsty and give you something to drink? 38 Or a stranger and show you hospitality? Or naked and give you clothing? 39 When did we ever see you sick or in prison and visit you?'

40 "And the King will say, 'I tell you the truth when you did it to one of the least of these my brothers and sisters, you were doing it to me!' (NLT)

Isn't that interesting? By giving ourselves to the welfare of others in works and prayers, Jesus says we were taking care of Him.

Today, write out names of people you'll be praying for their salvation, and fill the blank spaces in the prayers below with the names.

PRAYERS/DECLARATIONS

For Others' Salvation

O Lord, I Thank You because You do not want me, my family, my children, and these people I have here on my list to perish. Thank You, Lord, because You want us to be saved.

This is the assurance I have in You that as I pray, I receive answers, in Jesus name.

Today O Lord, I declare that these shall be saved and come to the knowledge of the truth in Christ Jesus.

Let Your power of salvation visit the following people, Lord. Visit ---------wherever they are right now. Visit them in the name of Jesus Christ.

Father Lord, I ask that out of Your unlimited resources, You will empower .... with the inner strength to accept Jesus as their Lord and Savior, in Jesus name.

Cause .... to be planted deep in the Love of Christ. Let them be rooted deep in Your love and comprehend with all of God's people the extravagant dimensions of Your love, in Jesus name.

Today, O Lord, I come against the spirit of rebellion in the lives of .... in Jesus name.

I cast out every spirit of stubbornness and resistance; I command these anti-salvation spirits to be drowned in the abyss in the Mighty name of Jesus Christ.

Satan, I speak to you as one with authority from God to stop your works here on earth. I command you to lose your grips in the lives of .... right now, in Jesus name.

Wherever you are................, I decree today that Jesus sets free; you are therefore free indeed. You are no longer under the influence of satan and sin, in Jesus name.

I command .... to receive an encounter with Jesus Christ today. Receive a supernatural revelation of the person of Christ and be rooted in His Love subsequently, in the name of Jesus.

O Lord, my Father, I confess that............. are saved and serving You, in Jesus name.

For the Sick

How God anointed Jesus of Nazareth with the Holy Ghost and with power: who went about doing good and healing all that were oppressed of the devil; for God was with him - **Acts 10:38**

Dear heavenly Father,

It is Your will to heal us and for us to walk in divine health. The price for our healing has been paid on the cross by Your Son, Jesus Christ.

So Father, as I pray for.......this day, I am confident that Your healing power will be made manifest for their healing and deliverance from the sickness and pain tormenting them, in Jesus name.

O Lord, I stand in the gap now and ask for forgiveness for ....

By the Blood of Jesus, I claim forgiveness from any sin and disobedience that has brought or empowered sickness to operate in the lives of......... in Jesus name.

According to Your Word, Lord, you forgive our sins and heal our diseases (Psalm 103:3). Therefore, I ask for forgiveness and total healing for .... in Jesus name.

I speak to the demons perpetrating sickness in the lives of ....

I command you demons to get out of their bodies this moment and be drowned in the abyss, in Jesus name.

As it is written, our bodies are the temple of the Holy Spirit. The bodies of .... are the temple of the Holy Spirit.

Therefore, you demons of affliction, pain, and defilement, pack your loads and leave now. I cast you all into the bottomless pit, in Jesus name.

I declare the bodies of .... as the temples of the Holy Spirit. I anoint them with oil now and decree complete healing and restoration of health, in the name of Jesus Christ.

O Lord, I ask that angels will carry out a spiritual surgery on .... today and bring them total healing.

I decree that .... will prosper and be in good health, even as their soul prospers in the Lord, from today, in Jesus name.

Amen.

REMEMBER THIS...

If you're confused about what God is calling you to do, start by accepting that you have received a ministry of reconciliation from Him.

DAY 18

PRATERS FOR THE NATION

---

1 Timothy 2:1-2 — ₁I urge, then, first of all, that petitions, prayers, intercession, and thanksgiving be made for all people — ₂for kings and all those in authority, that we may live peaceful and quiet lives in all godliness and holiness."

Today, let's pray for our nation, state, and community. While we may not have the connections to look at our politicians and reps in the face and rebuke them, our prayers can go a long way in helping to shape our land.

The Bible says, *"If my people, which are called by my name, shall humble themselves, and pray, and seek my face, and turn from their wicked ways; then will I hear from heaven, and will forgive their sin, and will heal their land (2 Chron 7:14).*

Our prayers can provoke divine intervention in our political and economic landscape. And until there is a supernatural intervention in the land, there will be no breakthrough for the Church.

> Pray for peace in Jerusalem. May all who love this city prosper - Psalm 122:6 (NLT)

Our country, states, cities, and neighborhoods represents our Jerusalem. If there is no peace in the land, we will be affected.

Fortunately, God says that if we pray for the land, He will heal the land, give us breakthrough and cause us to possess the land spiritually, and excel in it.

Yes, there are times I feel it's a waste praying for my country, especially when physical events in politics do not reflect our prayers. I find myself struggling, wondering why politicians can deceive us, play on our intelligence, loot our shared heritage, and walk away boldly without punishment.

I'm sure I'm not the only Christian who struggles many times with the idea of praying for our politicians. But we can encourage ourselves, knowing that God is working things out for our good even when physical events don't say so.

Our nations desperately need the life-giving renewal and redemption that flow from Christ's life, death, and resurrection.

PRAYERS/DECLARATIONS

Father, in the name of Jesus Christ, I thank You for making me a part of this community and neighborhood. Thank You for making me a citizen of this country.

It was not by accident that You brought me to live and work in this place. So I praise Your name forever and ever, in Jesus name.

O Lord, according to Your Word, my light will continue to shine in this land and will never be hidden. I will be an example of righteousness and the blessings of God in this community, in Jesus name.

I decree that the lamp of my salvation will never be put out in this land. Whatever is working to put out my light in this community, O Lord, frustrate them, in Jesus name.

Any evil spirit claiming ownership of this land and working against God's people and the Gospel, I overthrow you and cast you into the abyss, in Jesus name.

I break all forms of resistance against the prayers of believers in this land.

Let the warring angels of heaven be released and oppose all spiritual oppositions causing blockades for believers' prayers in this community and neighborhood and begin to hasten answers to all prayers, in Jesus name.

I raise the banner of victory over this city and declare that Jesus Christ is the Lord and ruler of this land, in Jesus name.

By the Blood of Jesus Christ, I command all demonic prison doors holding men and women from coming to the knowledge of Christ to be destroyed right now, in Jesus name.

Holy Spirit, move in this community and convict men, women, and children to accept Jesus Christ as their Lord and Savior, in Jesus name.

Father, I pray for the peace and prosperity of this neighborhood and this nation. May the inhabitants of this neighborhood and community come to the knowledge of Jesus Christ. May they prosper, and may peace be within the walls of this land, in Jesus name.

O Lord, may the Light of the Gospel shine deep in this land, and may darkness be leveled completely, in Jesus name.

Every witchcraft and python spirit afflicting this neighborhood and community, I bind and cast you into the abyss, in Jesus name.

I tear down all strongholds in and surrounding this town/city. I bind and rebuke them and command them to be destroyed in Jesus name.

Father Lord, I lift my country before thee. I pray that Your Love will prevail in all the land, and Your knowledge will reign supreme over all flesh, in Jesus name.

I break every curse that has been put against this community, its inhabitants, the county, and the state of [name] by persons living or dead, in Jesus name.

I claim victory over the city and town of [name], I claim victory over the county of [name], I claim victory over the state of [name], and all inhabitants thereof, in the name of Jesus Christ.

I plead the blood of Jesus Christ over this land, and I station angels in all the four corners of this community. I declare that the will of God will be done in this land, in Jesus name.

I expel the spirit of baal and false worship in the state and this nation. May all the prophets of baal in this land be exposed, in Jesus name.

I pull down all strongholds and altars of baal and ashtaroth established in any part of this neighborhood, community, state, and nation. I command all the operations of baal and the prophets to cease in Jesus name.

You spirits of mammon and molech that have invaded the Church, I bind you all this day, and I command all your operations in the Church to cease, in Jesus name.

O Lord, intervene in Your church. Expose all the evil operators that are causing reproach to the name of Christ. Send us revival and glorify the name of Your Son, Jesus Christ, in Jesus name.

Thank You, Heavenly Father, for answered prayers, in Jesus name.

Amen.

REMEMBER THIS...

"Our prayers can provoke divine intervention in our political and economic landscape."

DAY 19

CHOOSE TO WALK IN FORGIVENESS

1 Samuel 30: 21-24 ₂₁ David came to the two hundred men who were so exhausted that they could not follow him and had been left at the brook Besor with the provisions. They went out to meet David and the people with him, and when he approached the people, he greeted them.

₂₂ Then all the wicked and worthless men among those who went with David said, "Because they did not go with us, we will give them none of the spoil that we have recovered, except that each man may take his wife and children away and leave."

₂₃ David said, "You must not do so, my brothers, with what the Lord has given us. He has kept us safe and has handed over to us the band of Amalekites that came against us.

₂₄ And who will listen to you regarding this matter? For as is the share of him who goes down into the battle, so shall his share be who stays by the provisions and supplies; they shall share alike."

Thi is a very moving story. David refused to pay evil with evil. He forgave and distributed the spoils equally to everyone.

These men had wanted to stone him earlier on for an offense he did not commit. He encouraged himself in the Lord, mustered the strength to chase the enemy. The men did not join him in the chase. But when God gave him victory, he still thought to share the spoils with them.

That's the key to consistently winning with God: You must forgive offenses as quickly as possible and move on to stay in the will and blessings of God for your life.

The Bible says:

> Whenever you stand to pray, forgive if you have anything against anyone so that your Father, who is in heaven, will also forgive you your transgressions. But if you do not forgive, neither will your Father who is in heaven forgive your transgressions - Mark 11:25-26

It won't be easy to practice forgiveness, especially when we consider the scale of the offenses. However, if we're going to stay in the will of God and manifest His blessings for our lives, we must embrace forgiveness. From time to time, we must come before God and prayerfully forgive all offenses and let God take control.

When we choose to walk in forgiveness this way, we accept people's fallibility and not trust too much. We are giving room never to allow people's negative interpretations and reactions towards us to choke the love of God in our lives. We're telling ourselves, say, *"Hey, come what may, there's no room for anger, bitterness, depression, and other negative feelings in my life."*

Someone said, "Unforgiveness is like drinking poison yourself and waiting for the other person to die."

And you know what, she's right.

Unforgiveness does more harm to us than the offenders. It is like serving a prison term for the offense of someone else. That's why I encourage people to practice *advance forgiveness*.

As the year progresses, mistakes will be made, and offenses will come. But resolving to move on ahead of time will energize you to overcome the urge to fight back when these attacks occur.

There is nothing unforgivable, and there are no pains that our God cannot help you overcome. Sit down, pray, and say, "Lord, help me to do this. Help me to forgive."

HOW TO LOVE IN A LOVELESS WORLD

As we prepare to wrap up this prayer retreat, I would like to challenge you to give love in a loveless world. No matter how irritating people act towards you, choose love.

You say, "I want to love Daniel, but...

- "How do you give love where and when you were given hate?

- "How do you love those who betrayed you?

- "How do you love family members who spread lies about you?

- "How do you love people who are complicit in the death of your loved one?

- "How do you love brothers who sold you into slavery?

- "How do you love someone who walked out of the marriage, leaving you with four children to care for without any assistance?

- "How do you love those who hate you?

- "I mean, how?

Let's start by reading up what Jesus said:

> "You have heard that it was said, 'Love your neighbor and hate your enemy.' But I tell you, love your enemies and pray for those who persecute you, that you may be children of your Father in heaven. He causes his sun to rise on the evil and the good and sends rain on the righteous and the unrighteous. If you love those who love you, what reward will you get? Are not even the tax collectors doing that?

> And if you greet only your own people, what are you doing more than others? Do not even pagans do that? - Matthew 5: 43-47

First and foremost, Jesus doesn't mean that if someone is toxic and drains your energy, you should remain in the relationship so that you can prove that you love your enemy. He doesn't mean that if someone is killing you, you should let them do so just because you are trying to love the person. If you die, you won't have the chance to love

In this text, Jesus referred to an existing system that promoted an eye for an eye. His message was simple: "Leave vengeance for God. Let God fight for you. Don't do an eye for an eye."

> *So, your first step in loving those who hate you is accepting not to take revenge. Let God fight for you. He will do it in a better way.*

But how do you handle the emotions, the pains, and the sufferings? What should you do when it's hard to let go and when the people are not repentant?

1. Acknowledge the Pain You Feel

There are times that you want to move on, but you just don't know how. I mean, you can see the people who hurt you enjoying their lives, and the pastor says, move on. You want to do so. But how do you do that?

First things first: Acknowledge the pain you feel. Don't pretend about it with some sweet, motivating, positive confessions. Come to God as you are and tell Him how you feel. Be honest with Him.

2. Ask God for Grace

I had a terrible experience that gave me an accurate picture of the story of Joseph. My experience made me understand the depth of the pains he suffered when his brothers betrayed him and sold him into slavery.

Forgiving people who deliberately and relentlessly hurt you is tough, especially if these people were close to you and you trusted them. It is even more challenging when they seem to enjoy their lives while you seem to be suffering. However, we can pray for grace and the power to forgive.

When you're struggling with letting go, continue to ask God for grace to forgive and love. Tell Him that You are finding it difficult, but You are willing to stick with His Word. Keep praying like this:

> "Lord, my feelings are telling me to take revenge. My feelings are telling me to fight back. And yes, Lord, I want to fight back. I do feel I should not just take all this rubbish.

> "But Lord, I want to obey Your Word. I know that my feelings can be wrong, but Your Word is always right. Therefore, Lord, help me to forgive and love. I don't know how it will be done, but I trust You to help me, in Jesus name.

3. Believe that Something Good Will Come Out in the End

Joseph could not fathom how slavery and imprisonment were part of the process of fulfilling the vision of greatness God gave him. But in God's plan, the entire trial, although carried out by satan, ended up bringing God's plan to pass.

God uses what we call satan's smartness and attacks to establish His glory and bring about His promises. So yes, something good will come out of whatever negative situation we find ourselves.

We may not know how it will happen. We may not see where everything is taking us to. We may not even understand the whole mess. We may feel perplexed or feel like taking a break from our faith. We may be counting our losses and shame. But one thing is sure: something good will come out of the situation. That is what the Word of God says, and that is what will happen.

So, look beyond the insults and see the glory. Look beyond the offenses and see the testimony. Look beyond the misrepresentations and see the breakthrough. Look beyond the betrayals and see the blessings. God will use everything the enemy intends for evil to establish His victory in your life.

4. Don't Blame Yourself Too Much

When I had an experience of betrayal, it was hard stopping to blame myself. Almost every night, I kept asking myself, "How could I be so senseless? Why didn't I suspect this kind of thing at all? How could I be here, and they defrauded me with my eyes wide open? How could I be so stupidly trusting?"

I battled with self-blames until I sensed God dropping the following words in my heart: *"Don't blame yourself too much for another person's mischief."*

The people who hurt others will often attempt to blame their victims. For instance, a cheating spouse will say things like, *"You were not there when I needed you."* A stealing business partner will say, *"I needed money to complete my rent. You did not support me when I asked for your help."*

But learn never to blame yourself for another person's foolishness. We are all responsible for our actions. Instead of blaming yourself too much, ask God to teach you profound truths about the hearts of humans.

5. Give Yourself Time to Heal

If I forgive, will the hurt I feel go away?

Of course, not immediately. But forgiveness has nothing to do with feelings. Forgiveness is a decision. Healing is a process.

When I say, "I forgive," it's instant. But the pain I feel will take time to be healed.

So when you still feel some pains even after saying you forgive, don't feel bad. Nothing is wrong with you. Healing is a process, and at times it can take some time. Continue to cry out to God from your heart. You'll be healed and strengthened. And you'll become better and better.

6. Ask for Counsel, But Don't Follow Every Advice

When you've been hurt, you will find yourself needing counsel and asking for people's opinions here and there. It's good to receive all the advice you can get. The Bible says that in the multitude of counseling, there is safety. But beware of the final advice you choose to follow. Why?

When I found myself in a complicated situation to let go of an offense, I cried out to many counselors and experts and received different suggestions. And these suggestions seemed like the perfect thing to do in all the books. But as I prayed and listened to my heart, I sensed that what these experts were saying was not what I should do. I saw in my spirit God asking me to follow a different direction.

Sometimes, the spirit of lies and deception can use experts to get to us. Not because they do not know what they are saying, but because at that particular time, their counsel is not the will of God for the situation at hand. You'll need a lot of humility and patience to see what should be done through the Holy Spirit.

> *Today, declare that you chose to love and forgive no matter what and be willing to forgive yourself and others for any pain they have caused you.*

Chose to walk in love and let every anger and bitterness go. It's not easy, especially when you consider the scale of the issue in question.

However, if God can forgive us of our deepest and darkest sins, we need to forgive others as well.

Don't forget: we do not forgive because the persons involved have repented and apologized. We forgive because that's the only way to set ourselves free from their cage and connect to our blessings.

PRAYERS/DECLARATIONS

For the Fruit of the Holy Spirit

Heavenly Father,

Thank You for engrafting me in Christ Jesus by the Holy Spirit as a branch. You designed me to bear fruit of righteousness, love, peace, joy, gentleness, self-control, goodness, patience, and kindness.

O Lord, I desire to bear these fruits in my life.

I desire to remain rooted in Christ, bearing fruit that leads others to the light of God's love.

I desire to walk in LOVE, forgiving others at all times, and gifting God's blessings on my life with others, just as God loved and gave Jesus to die for us.

I desire, every day, to walk in joy, peace, gentleness, self-control, goodness, patience, and kindness so that I will be an example that brings others to Christ. Help me, empower me, and teach me to bear Your fruit every day in Jesus name.

Holy Spirit, I desire to walk in peace with myself and with others as a child of God.

I desire to walk in patience, for faith makes no haste.

I desire to walk in kindness, thoughtfulness, and compassion for others, just as Christ was compassionate at all times.

Provide me with daily assistance to bear these fruits of peace, patience, and kindness in abundance so that Jesus will be glorified in my life every day, in Jesus name.

Holy Spirit, I desire to bear the fruit of goodness so that I may lead others to Jesus Christ.

I desire to be faithful at all times with whatever God blesses me with so that I may stand before God in the end and receive the rewards of faithfulness.

I desire to be gentle with myself and others in thoughts, words, and actions so that I may be an instrument of encouragement and uplifting to others and not discouragement.

I desire to walk in self-control in food, dressing, and in everything so that I can win the race set before me and not be cast away after preaching to others.

I call upon You to empower me every day to bear these fruits as I live, serve God, and relate with others, in Jesus name, I pray.

Amen.

REMEMBER THIS...

Your first step in loving those who hate you is accepting not to take revenge. God will fight for you, and He will do it in a better way.

DAY 20

WAKE UP YOUR GIFTS

Ephesians 2:10 - For we are God's handiwork, created in Christ Jesus to do good works, which God prepared in advance for us to do (NIV).

If we will walk in prevail in all circumstances this year, we must awaken our gifts. Our gifts are God's tools in us to work His works.

God blessed us all with powerful gifts, which, if used, will empower us to excel in the world irrespective of the darkness in it. That is why our prayer today focuses on awakening God's gifts, skills, and talents in our lives.

Make these declarations as we proceed:

- I am God's creation

- I am fearfully and wonderfully made

- I am created in Christ Jesus

- I am created to do good works

- I am blessed with powerful gifts and skills

- This year, God will use my gifts and abilities for His glory, in Jesus name.

If we all functioned in our gifts, the world would be so afraid of us because of how we excel. Unfortunately, we seem to be struggling to get our daily needs met that we don't even have time to question the gifts and skills God gave us. We end up like the guy in Jesus' parable who went and hid his talent out of fear.

Life does not end in getting your daily bread and being happy in marriage. Today, pray from the depth of your heart for the reawakening of your gifts. Let your gifts speak so loud this year that God will be glorified

MEDITATE ON THESE SCRIPTURES

Matthew 25: 14-30 (MSG) - It's also like a man going off on an extended trip. He called his servants together and delegated responsibilities. To one, he gave five thousand dollars to another two thousand, to a third one thousand, depending on their abilities. Then he left. Right off, the first servant went to work and doubled his master's investment. The second did the same. But the man with the single thousand dug a hole and ....

1 Peter 4:10-11 (ESV) - ₁₀As each has received a gift, use it to serve one another, as good stewards of God's varied grace: 11 whoever speaks, as one who speaks oracles of God; whoever serves, as one who serves by the strength that God supplies—in order that in everything God may be glorified through Jesus Christ. To him belong glory and dominion forever and ever. Amen.

Romans 12:1-21 (ESV) - I appeal to you, therefore, brothers, by the mercies of God, to present your bodies as a living sacrifice, holy and acceptable to God, which is your spiritual worship. Do not be conformed to this world, but be transformed by the renewal of your mind, that by testing you may discern what the will of God is, what is good and acceptable and perfect.

PRAYERS/DECLARATIONS

Heavenly Father, give me the wisdom to recognize the gifts and talents you have blessed me with. Grant me opportunities and open doors this year to put my gifts into profitable use, for Your kingdom's advancement, and my betterment, in Jesus name.

I pray that all my buried and undiscovered gifts will begin to manifest.

This year, I will bear fruits that bring glory to Jesus Christ, for God has called me to bear fruits.

I will not be barren.

My life will be fruitful, both spiritually and physically.

Through my gifts and skills, God's kingdom will go forward.

Through my gifts, my generation will be blessed, in Jesus name.

In the name of Jesus Christ, I decree that I will not leave this world without making use of all the gifts and callings that God has given to me.

This world will be blessed through my life, gifts, and talents in Jesus name.

May every attack on my gifts and skills, designed to frustrate and keep me unfulfilled cease today, in the name of Jesus Christ.

I command all my gifts, skills, and talents to wake up from this day forward and begin to speak loud and clear.

I command every spirit of fear and indiscipline projected to keep my gifts and skills from speaking out, to lose their grips on me.

I set myself free from all forms of limitations against my gifts and abilities and decree that I will henceforth excel in what God has empowered me to do and become, in Jesus name.

Father, I recognize that You are the creator and giver of all good gifts. May I only become what You have designed me to become, and may my gifts and skills glorify Your name.

Today, and onwards, I receive grace, wisdom, and strength to labor on the gifts and talents that I have received from God, in Jesus name.

Amen.

Rehoboth 2022

REMEMBER THIS…

"If we all functioned in our gifts, the world would be so afraid of us because of how we excel."

DAY 21

SAY NO TO THE ANGEL OF DEATH

Psalm 91: 16 - With long life will God satisfy you, and show you His salvation

---

This year, God wants you to prevail over death. Nothing can kill you before your divinely appointed time.

A man of God once said, *"Even if the devil is the driver of the vehicle I boarded, he will take me to my destination."*

Don't fold your arms and say, "Well, what will be will be." That's not how to prevail and enter your Rehoboth.

This year, say no to the spirit of death. Don't accept what God is against.

God wants you to live a long and healthy life. Premature death is not part of His plans for you. Read the following scriptures:

- Proverbs 3:1-2,
- Proverbs 18: 21,
- Psalm 34:12-14,
- Psalm 91: 14-16

As you can see, long life is God's will, and we have a road map to help us:

- Keep your tongue from negativity,
- Don't tell lies,
- Depart from evil,
- Do good to others,
- Seek and pursue peace,
- Love the Lord,
- Obey the voice of the Holy Spirit

The good thing is that these directions are not grievous. Through the Holy Spirit's help, we can walk with God and obey His Words.

Today, pass a decree against the spirits and powers of death and remind God of His promise to preserve your life.

You will not die. You will live and declare the goodness of God.

PRAYERS/DECLARATIONS

Father Lord, I thank You for the promise of long life to those who obey You. I praise and magnify Your name, this day, and forever, in Jesus name.

Lord, I commit the totality of my life into Your hands this year and beyond; help me by the Holy Spirit to walk in Your ways and to keep Your instructions.

Engrave Your fear in my heart every day, for it is written that the fear of the Lord prolongs days (Prov. 10:27).

Holy Spirit, empower me to obey and serve You every day so that I may spend my days in prosperity and my years in joy and strength (Job 36:11).

Plant the laws and commandments of God in my heart and help me never to forget them, and may they lengthen my days and cause me to dwell in peace and security, in Jesus name (Proverbs 3:1-2).

According to the Word of God, I declare that I shall not die but live and continue to proclaim the goodness of God (Psalm 118:17).

This year, no member of my family shall die.

We will fulfill the number of our years.

We will live to eat the fruit of our labor, for we shall not labor for another to enjoy, in Jesus name (Isaiah 65:23).

Today, I rebuke the spirit of death and cast it into the abyss. I decree that there shall be no mourning and shedding of tears in my family this year.

All through this year, I cover myself and my family with the Blood of Jesus Christ.

May the Blood of Jesus continue to speak in our favor, in Jesus name.

The Lord God Almighty will satisfy us with long life, and under His wings shall we find refuge, in Jesus name.

Thank You, Jesus, in Jesus name, I pray.

Amen

REMEMBER THIS...

Don't fold your arms and say, "Well, what will be will be." That's not how to prevail and enter your Rehoboth.

HALLELUJAH!

This is the confidence we have before Him: that if we ask anything according to His will, He hears us. And if we know that He hears and listens to us in whatever we ask, we have the assurance that He will grant our requests. – 1 John 5:14-15 (Paraphrased)

We began this prayer retreat with a gratitude check; let's also end it with praise and a reminder that God is answering our prayers.

There are times our minds may wonder if the prayers we have said, declared, and made makes any difference. Today, be assured that, yes, your prayers make a tremendous difference.

Your prayers are changing your situations and empowering you to win. They are making things to align to your favor and bring you into the fullness of God's purpose for your life.

> ***If God did not plan to answer our prayers, He would not have asked us to pray***

You may not have feelings of excitement; that's not a sign that something is wrong.

Don't judge your prayers based on how you feel. Our prayers are not answered based on our feelings.

The Scripture we read today says once we have prayed according to God's will, that is, according to the **word of God**, that we have answers to our prayers. This means that all the prayers and declarations we have prayed and declared in the last twenty-one days are getting the desired responses. They are speaking for our victory.

What should we do next?

Simple. Spend time thanking God for every prayer you have said and every declaration you have made. Decree and declare your confidence in God's Word for your life.

This year, you will prevail in every area of your life. You will see supernatural interventions and restoration. You will grow and multiply.

It is your year of Rehoboth.

MEDITATE ON THESE SCRIPTURES...

Mark 11:24 - Therefore I say unto you, what things soever ye desire, when ye pray, believe that ye receive them, and ye shall have them.

1 John 5:14-15 - And this is the confidence that we have in him, that, if we ask anything according to his will, he hears us.

John 15:7 - If ye abide in me, and my words abide in you, ye shall ask what ye will, and it shall be done unto you.

Matthew 7:7 - Ask, and it shall be given you; seek, and ye shall find; knock, and it shall be opened unto you:

Jeremiah 33:3 - Call unto me, and I will answer thee, and shew thee great and mighty things, which thou knowest not.

1 John 3:22 - And whatsoever we ask, we receive of him, because we keep his commandments, and do those things that are pleasing in his sight.

Jeremiah 29:12 - Then shall ye call upon me, and ye shall go and pray unto me, and I will hearken unto you.

Hebrews 11:1 - Now faith is the substance of things hoped for, the evidence of things not seen.

PRAYERS/DECLARATIONS

Heavenly Father, I have called on You in these past days. I have offered many prayers and declarations and supplications. I am here today to declare that I believe, according to Thy Word, that You have answered my prayers.

O Lord, I prayed that strongholds causing barriers between me and Your blessings to be removed, and I thank You today because every stronghold in my life has been rolled away.

My family and I are no longer under any generational curse from this day forward because the curses have now been neutralized by the Blood of Jesus Christ, in Jesus name.

Monitoring demons over my life have been defeated, bound, and are now resting in the abyss until Jesus comes.

I am now followed by the angels of God, who are working to bring to pass God's plans for my life.

I have the spirit of boldness, love, power, and a sound mind.

Fear is defeated in my life forever and ever. I will take bold steps ordained by God to bring me into my place of testimony from now onwards, in Jesus name.

The powers of witchcraft over my life, family, business, career, destiny, and environment have been destroyed, and they will remain destroyed forever and ever.

From this day on, I am taking back hundred-fold whatever has been damaged in my life and destiny, in Jesus name

---

I declare that afflictions and infirmity are defeated in my life and family and in the lives of my loved ones whom I have prayed for. The healing power of God is at work in my life and that of my loved ones from this day forward, in Jesus name.

Lord, I declare that my marriage and home are blessed. We are enjoying divine favor every day, in Jesus name.

I am God's sheep. I hear His voice, and I follow Him. So, I do not lack His direction. This year, I will make the right decisions in every aspect of my life, and I will enjoy peace and progress in Jesus name.

O Lord, I take the full recovery of all my stolen blessings in the past. My family and I have total victory over the devil and his works. We have complete restoration and dominion in every area of our lives, in Jesus name.

This year, even if darkness and gross darkness cover the earth, God's glory will be seen in my life, every day, every week, every month, and in every place I go, in Jesus name.

ANOINT YOURSELF AND PRAY

Heavenly Father, I anoint myself today; I anoint my house, and I anoint this environment and completely surrender and dedicate everything to You.

I declare that my life, my family, and this place shall be holy unto You.

Just as Jesus was anointed with Holy Ghost and with power and He went about doing good and healing all who were oppressed by the devil, I also pray that my life, my family, and this house and environment shall be a source from which good news, healing, encouragement, light, and favor shall flow through to others, in Jesus name.

Thank you, Lord, for doing unto me as you have heard me speak into your ears, in Jesus name.

PRAISE GOD

Since this is the last prayer day in our New Year prayer retreat, just praise God. Bring God an offering of praise and worship. Sing and dance before Him, for He has given you victory.

Hallelujah!

CLOSING DECLARATION

I have the life of God in me.

I have His wisdom and strength working on the inside of me.

I can do all things through Christ, who strengthens me.

I have understanding, strength, and divine direction.

I am not a confused fellow overwhelmed with life and circumstances.

I am in complete control of life and everything that comes my way, for the Holy Spirit, my Senior Partner, will always guide me on what to do and how to proceed, at all times and in all circumstances, in Jesus name.

Amen.

SOMETHING GOOD IS ON YOUR WAY

- Dr Daniel Okpara

GET IN TOUCH

We love testimonies. So, please share how this book or other of my books has inspired or helped you. Connect with me on social media:

Facebook: www.facebook.com/drdanielokpara

Instagram: @drdanielokpara

Telegram: https://t.me/mybetterlifetoday

Also, consider checking out my other books on Amazon:

amazon.com/author/danielokpara .

Visit our website, www.BetterLifeWorld.org, and send us your prayer request. As we join faith with you, God's power will be made manifest in your life.

BOOKS BY THE SAME AUTHOR

LATEST BOOKS

Prayers to Cancel Disappointments at the Edge of Breakthrough

Prayers to Cancel the Curse of Marital Delay

Prayers to Remove Yourself from Negative Generational Patterns

31 Days in the School of Faith

31 Days With the Heroes of Faith

31 Days With the Holy Spirit

31 Days With Jesus

31 Days in the Parables

None of These Diseases

I Will Arise and Shine

Psalm 91

ALL BOOKS

Prayer Retreat:
HEALING PRAYERS & CONFESSIONS
200 Violent Prayers
Hearing God's Voice in Painful Moments

Healing Prayers

Healing WORDS

Prayers That Break Curses

120 Powerful Night Prayers

How to Pray for Your Children Everyday

How to Pray for Your Family

Daily Prayer Guide

Make Him Respect You

How to Cast Out Demons from Your Home, Office & Property

Praying Through the Book of Psalms

The Students' Prayer Book

How to Pray and Receive Financial Miracle

Powerful Prayers to Destroy Witchcraft Attacks.

Deliverance from Marine Spirits

Deliverance From Python Spirit

Anger Management God's Way

How God Speaks to You

Deliverance of the Mind

20 Commonly Asked Questions About Demons

Praying the Promises of God

When God Is Silent

I SHALL NOT DIE

Praise Warfare

Prayers to Find a Godly Spouse

How to Exercise Authority Over Sickness

Under His Shadow

AUDIOBOOKS

120 Powerful Night Prayers that Will Change Your Life

28 Days of Praise Challenge

Anger Management God's Way

By His Stripes

Deliverance of the mind

Healing Words: Daily Confessions & Declarations

How God Speaks to You

How to Exercise Authority Over Sickness

How to Meditate on God's Word

Prayers to Find a Godly Spouse

Praying the Promises of God

Take it By Force

Under His Shadow

When God Is Silent

Besides the Still Waters

Less Panic More Hope

How to Pray for Your Family

Prayers that Break Curses

20 Commonly Asked Questions About Demons

Deliverance by Fire

Command Your Money

ABOUT THE AUTHOR

Daniel Chika Okpara is an influential voice in contemporary Christian ministry. His mandate is to make lives better by teaching and preaching God's Word with signs and wonders. He is the resident pastor of Shining Light Christian Centre, a fast-growing church in Lagos.

He is also the president and CEO of Better Life World Outreach Center, a non-denominational ministry dedicated to global evangelism, prayer revival, and empowering God's people with the WORD to make their lives better. Through his Breakthrough Prayers Foundation (www.breakthroughprayers.org), an online portal leading people worldwide to encounter God and change their lives through prayer, thousands of people encounter God through prayer, and hundreds of testimonies are received from all around the world.

As a foremost Christian teacher and author, his books are in high demand in prayer groups, Bible studies, and personal devotions. He has authored over 80 life-transforming books and manuals on business, prayer, relationship, and victorious living, many of which have become international best-sellers.

He is a Computer Engineer by training and holds a master's degree in Christian Education from Continental Christian University. He is married to Doris Okpara, his friend and they are blessed with lovely children.

WEBSITE: www.betterlifeworld.org

FREE BOOKS

To appreciate you for obtaining this book, I'm offering you these four powerful books today for free. Download them on our website and take your relationship with God to a new level.

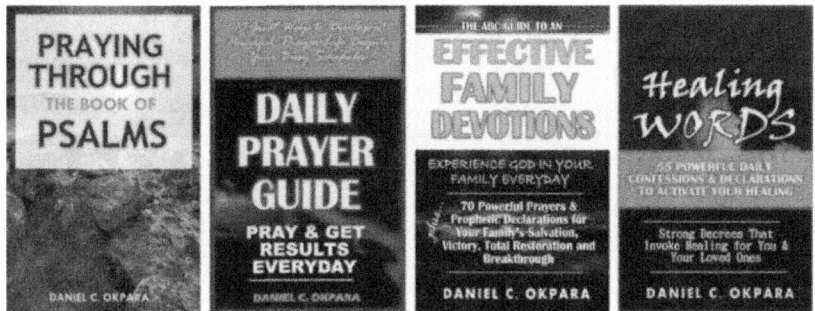

<u>Click Here to Download</u>

<u>www.betterlifeworld.org/grow</u>

NOTES

Made in the USA
Coppell, TX
25 June 2022

79227382R00215